THE
SALES
CONTRARIAN

THE
SALES
CONTRARIAN

Opening the Minds of
Salespeople and Sales Leaders
for the Greater Good

Steve Heroux

RIVER GROVE
BOOKS

Published by River Grove Books
Austin, TX
www.rivergrovebooks.com

Distributed by River Grove Books

Design and composition by Greenleaf Book Group and Brian Phillips
Cover design by Greenleaf Book Group and Adrian Morgan
Cover images copyright Dotted Yeti, ismail19797, and Michal Sanca.
Used under license from Shutterstock.com

Publisher's Cataloging-in-Publication data is available.

Print ISBN: 978-1-63299-863-7

eBook ISBN: 978-1-63299-864-4

First Edition

CONTENTS

WHY I WROTE THIS BOOK

THIS BOOK IS AN INVITATION TO BREAK FREE from the constraints of the past and embrace a new era of dynamic, empowered, and ethical leadership. It's about recognizing that the old ways are no longer effective and that a revolution in thought and practice is not just necessary but inevitable. These outdated methods, born in a different era, have hindered growth, stifled innovation, and left many feeling powerless in their professional journeys. Way too many organizations have discarded talented salespeople and refused to adapt to today's business climate. Fostering nurturing environments and providing psychological safety have practically been eradicated. But times have changed. The world has evolved, and so must our approach to leading and selling.

As a self-proclaimed (and often accused) contrarian, I can assure you that some of what you are about to read will cause you to think I was raised next to a power plant, ate paint chips as a kid, or multiple screws are loose inside my head. All of that may be true; however, I do have some rational thoughts cross my mind every now and then. Sue me for thinking that salespeople don't want to be treated like a number. Laugh at me for believing that salespeople should not be instructed to sell to anyone who draws breath and is willing to give them money. Call me crazy for thinking that all training should be customized and built specifically for the individual, instead of teaching a one-size-fits-all "magic" selling methodology to everyone.

This book is intended to lead a charge, incite a movement, and advance us all forward toward victory in both business and life. It's about adopting modern practices that cultivate growth, inspire teams, and drive genuine success. Whether you're a seasoned sales leader or just starting your sales career, this book will equip you with the tools you need to lead with integrity, sell with passion, and achieve unparalleled results. But hey, I'm crazy, remember?

1

DISPELLING THE MYTHS ABOUT SELLING

I REMEMBER BEING TOLD SO MANY THINGS I should do if I wanted to be successful in sales. Most of the sales managers I worked under intended to help me sell more stuff, but in reality, it caused me to sell less stuff. It seemed like good advice at the time. However, it was misleading at best. I'm sure many of you had similar experiences, and it's okay to admit you were misled—I was too.

The endless list of bad advice could fill up an entire chapter. I'll save you the time and summarize my least favorite "nuggets of wisdom" and end with the worst piece of advice I've ever received in sales. I was told, "Leave no stone unturned and sell to everyone you can." I was told, "Don't stop calling until they tell you to stop calling or until you get a NO." I was told, "Time kills all deals." I was told, "You have to assume the close." I was told, "Sales is a numbers game." I was told, "Follow the script word for word." I was told, "Relationships are the key to selling." And the absolute, most abhorrent, disdainful, antiquated, morally void piece of advice I ever received was, "Always be closing."

I know you may be thinking, "How does he not believe in closing?! It's ABC, baby! Always be closing!" Even typing out those words makes my skin crawl and my innards curl up into a ball, and I'm sorry to burst your bubble if you're a self-proclaimed "closer."

Here's a tip: Having a "closer" attitude makes other people's skin crawl. Your prospects, customers, clients, teammates, employees, friends, families, and pretty much anyone with a soul are put off by this display of egomaniacal bravado.

If you're unaware of how this repugnant sales practice became popularized, it started in 1992. It was, unfortunately, brought to life by the movie *Glengarry Glen Ross*. Here's a quick overview based on Wikipedia's summary of the film: Four real estate salesmen are given low-quality leads by their office manager. They use unethical and high-pressure sales tactics to try to convince their targets to invest in new land developments. The company they work for sends the top salesman, Blake (played by Alec Baldwin), to motivate the four underperforming salesmen. Blake chides, insults, and verbally abuses the team, telling them that only the top performers will still have a job at the end of the month.[1]

It gets worse from there. Sounds like a wonderful environment in which to work. (I hope my sarcasm is leaping off the page here.)

Baldwin's character, Blake, is the epitome of a high-powered, low-empathy, egomaniacal, money-hungry salesperson who uses fear, intimidation, insults, and profanity-laced tirades to display his dominance. He says, "Because only one thing counts in this life—get them to sign on the line which is dotted. You hear me, you f**king f*****s." And after he continues to berate, emasculate, humiliate, and terrorize a group of his fellow salesmen, he utters the phrase that has collectively cost companies *trillions* of dollars in lost sales: "Always be closing. *Always* be closing."

Here's the scariest part, and I really want you to pay attention because this is not a joke. What he says next is what some sales managers say, think, do, and display. They may not say it verbatim, but this is what salespeople hear: "Nice guy? I don't give a s**t. Good father? F**k you! Go home and play with your kids! You wanna work here? Close!"[2]

Some of you reading this right now have had the wonderful and uplifting experience of working with sales managers exactly like this, if not worse, and I'm sorry to bring up horrible memories for you. For years, sales managers have subjected too many salespeople to this kind of behavior, which has become quite normal in many industries.

Sales leaders, managers, and some company owners watched this movie, witnessed this horrendous behavior, and said to themselves, "I love it! That's precisely who I want to be, and I can't wait to talk to my salespeople like this and duplicate this arrogance and self-loathing and display my superiority complex." I wish I were joking. Other sales managers thought to themselves, "Wow! This type of treatment will definitely build self-confidence in my salespeople. It will inspire them to reach greater heights. They'll be so much more effective, and I'm sure this is exactly what they're looking for in a sales leader." Obviously, this line of thinking is abundantly idiotic, and even fathoming that this type of mistreatment of salespeople will somehow inspire incredible results defies all semblance of reality.

This is precisely why the average consumer, for decades, has hated salespeople with a passion and thought of them as vile and loathsome. Many consumers feel like this because some salespeople think they're

God's gift to the world and that the only thing in life that matters is closing someone. (Puke noise.)

If you're in the world of sales in any capacity (sales, sales management, business ownership), you've been subjected to this closing garbage a million times. According to Blake from *Glengarry Glen Ross* (and way too many salespeople and sales managers), it doesn't matter who the prospect is, what their needs are, or whether what you're selling is right for them—your job is to close the deal and extricate the money from your prospect's pocket, no matter what. In the '80s and '90s, this abhorrent approach may have worked on unsuspecting prospects who'd never see you again. But fast-forward to present times and today's economic climate and marketplace, and things are a lot different, thankfully. The sad part is that you still see these egomaniacal, money-hungry, soulless, ABC fake gurus who peddle their fool-proof selling systems, magic funnels, and Ponzi scheme–like real estate scams that they claim will put you on the path to riches by tomorrow. Hollywood and social media have glorified these grifters and made it easy for them to take advantage of the naïve and downtrodden.

Most people in sales know *The Wolf of Wall Street*, which is based on a self-absorbed, drug-fueled, Napoleonic felon who stole hundreds of millions of dollars from unsuspecting investors and still hasn't paid back all the people whose lives he destroyed by stealing from them. He's added to his repertoire of grifting, which includes selling his "expertise" on cryptocurrency, NFTs, AI, and who knows what else. Many salespeople also know the name of the morally corrupt "uncle" who will 10X your life because he spent $100M on social media to create a fake persona and fake social proof of his so-called success. Yet most human beings find him nauseating and repulsive, and he wouldn't last a second in a professional business setting. If you subscribe to the ABC mentality, you may look up to these charlatans, and that's your business, but I feel sad for you. The thought of these people influencing salespeople and sales managers makes me ill. Unfortunately, plenty of people get hoodwinked and bamboozled into thinking these frauds are worth listening to. If you want to watch a sales movie—based on a true story—about a man who personifies grit, guts, determination, ethics, family, and pure, unadulterated effort and desire, watch *The Pursuit of Happyness*. That's a *real* sales movie. The movie is based on the life of a man named Chris Gardner, but unfortunately, most people don't know his name (please look him up). If you know and like this movie, and if you want to build a reputation in sales based on integrity, honor, conscientiousness, self-awareness, and putting the needs of your clients first, then this book is for you.

I learned this way too late in my life. Just because someone wants to buy something from you, that does *not* mean you should sell it to them.

You should never sell something to someone who truly doesn't need what you're offering. They may want it, they may think they need it, but if you know for a fact deep down in your core that selling to them is not the right thing to do, it's okay to walk away. You've probably heard the phrase, "They're so good, they could sell ice to an Eskimo." Selling ice to an Eskimo doesn't make you a great salesperson, it makes you an asshole; especially when they can get unlimited amounts of ice for free. I'm imploring you, on behalf of all the other human beings who occupy this planet, to please *stop* doing this ABC crap immediately. It's not helping you sell more; it's causing you to sell less.

We could spend hours and hours talking about what not to do and how this closing mentality is costing you millions in lifetime income. But instead of wasting our time on that, I will share something important with you that will help you become a world-class sales professional. The best professionals in the world of sales don't have to ask for the sale as much as others do. Why? Because their prospects *ask them*! "What's the next step, Cheryl?" Or "When can we get started, Andre?"

This is why you should consider selling in a more conscientious and consultative way. Yes, I understand that sometimes you do need to ask for someone's business. But the balance of power has shifted away from us as salespeople, and now it favors the prospect. The amount of research, data, and information available today is unending, and prospects are more informed and savvier than ever. The high-pressure sales tactics and one-call close BS don't work anymore because most people know they don't have to buy what you're selling at this exact moment. They have a dozen other options, providers, and vendors that can probably provide something similar to what you provide.

Many salespeople still hold an antiquated belief that all you need to be successful in sales is the magic-selling system from sixty years ago, which teaches some of the worst selling techniques I've ever seen. Teaching salespeople to use a sales technique called an upfront contract is ridiculous. This is a technique used to manipulate a prospect into thinking that, for some unknown reason, they *must* decide to give you a yes or no answer today. What?! Is this real?! Yep. Maybe this works in hypothetical situations with fake prospects in unrealistic role-play situations, but it should never be used by a salesperson with a real prospect in a business setting.

Here's what the upfront contract taught by this "magic" selling system teaches salespeople to do. They instruct salespeople to ask questions like, "Sonia, can we at least decide right now that if you're interested, we'll move forward, and if you're not interested, you'll tell me no?"

I swear this is real! This is the stuff that's taught to salespeople, and their companies pay for it! It's like walking up to a stranger in a bar and saying, "My name is Steve, and before I waste my time talking to you, can we decide right now that if you like me, you'll take me back to your place, and if you're not interested in taking me home tonight, you'll tell me no?"

What in the world? Who would ever do this?! And if that is the case, then why would anyone with a pulse or a brain ever think this is somehow an effective way to start a sales conversation with a prospect?! You can agree or disagree with me, but try this upfront contract jargon in any part of your daily life, and let's see what happens.

Even worse than using these old-fashioned, ancient, and mindless selling techniques from sixty years ago is the use of manipulative closing questions that will, somehow—apparently through telepathy—make your prospects buy from you. Please. It's a joke. That's why people make fun of these idiotic closing questions like, "What can I do to put you in this car today, Mateo?" Or "Tamika, is there anything that would prevent us from moving forward?" Argh. Many of today's salespeople really do say things like this, and they think it works. I'm *begging* you *not to use* these techniques and this old-school manipulative language.

What should you say instead? Before I share that with you, you need to ask yourself the following questions first as a salesperson before you can confidently ask a potential customer, acquire a new customer, or land the deal:

- Do I fully understand the needs of my prospect?
- Do I fully understand how their business works?

- Do I fully understand the marketplace and their position in that marketplace?
- What are their aspirations for the business?
- What are the issues and challenges preventing them from achieving greater success?
- When do they want to fix these issues?
- How will staying the same impact their bottom line or their life?
- Am I confident we can help them?
- Are we the right and best fit for them?
- Are there any red flags preventing us from taking on this client?

These are all questions you need the answers to before you can attempt to ask for their business with confidence. Your prospects will have their questions about you, which they'll need to answer before they are ready to decide and be fully comfortable moving forward. The most effective way to do this is to *seed* your answers to their questions throughout your presentation and focus on building massive amounts of value. They'll be asking questions like this about you:

- Do I trust them?
- Do I like them?
- Do they understand my exact situation?
- Can they really help us?
- Are they an expert in their field?
- Is their company reputable?
- Are they worth what they charge?
- Can they make my life easier?

After you feel like you've answered these questions to their liking, it's time to ask for their business—but not by spouting off some imbecilic closing question. This part of the sales process is incredibly simple, yet most salespeople make it complicated. I'm going to teach you one simple and effective way of asking for a prospect's business. I learned this from an amazing sales leader I look up to. It's eight short words.

"So, where do we go from here, Sandy?"

It's straightforward, to the point, with no fluff or manipulation, and your prospect has only two ways to answer this. They'll either say, "Yes, let's do it" (or some version of approval), or they'll give you an objection to explain why they're not ready to buy right now. That's exactly what we want as salespeople! Either a yes or a reason why they're not ready yet, which helps us figure out where we need to provide more clarity. At this point, you can use this information to address their objections and better clarify your value to them before asking for their business. Please remember this: Closing is not about manipulation, applying pressure, or using condescending old-school tactics. If you focus on learning how to build massive amounts of value in your presentation, and you seed the answers to the questions your prospects are asking themselves about you, you'll be surprised at how many more deals you land, clients you acquire, and income you earn. Try it!

Goals Aren't Helping You as Much as You Think

I can sense your trepidation, and I can feel your eyebrows furrowing as you read that heading. I can hear you saying to yourself, "How can this be true? We *need* goals. We're supposed to *set* goals. We need to *track* our goals. We should *write down* our goals. They should all be *smart* goals."

Just because you've been told the same stuff about goals for the last twenty years doesn't make it true. In fact, much of what we believe to be true isn't true. We live our lives based on our belief systems, but in most of those cases, our beliefs are not based on fact. Once we have a belief, we tend to cling to it, even when it is untrue. It's like Dallas Cowboys fans, who still think they have "America's Team." They haven't won anything in more than thirty years, but they act like the Cowboys win the Super Bowl every year. (They don't, in case you're not a sports fan.)

These delusional beliefs are caused by confirmation bias, which is the tendency to seek out information that supports what we already believe. We tend to surround ourselves with messages that confirm our preexisting opinions. For example, in the United States, many conservatives get their news from Fox (which leans right), and many liberals get their news from CNN (which leans left). If you're positive that some magic closing question increases sales, and some fake guru posts some doctored-up testimonials claiming their acronym-driven sales methodology works wonders, you'll believe it to be true, even if it's not.

These behaviors protect us from having to change our beliefs. Unfortunately, they may also keep us steadfastly believing things that aren't true. Despite our best intentions, it's easy to subconsciously buy into beliefs that feel right, even though they're not. Take a second to think about something you believe to be true. You may find that, in many cases, it's not actually true.

Columbus didn't discover America. Sorry, nope. Native Americans were here way before he "discovered" their land.

Napoleon Bonaparte was short. Sorry, nope, also not true. He was five feet six inches tall, which was the average height for men around the turn of the nineteenth century.

Sharks are blood-thirsty killers. Sorry, nope, this one's not even close to being true. Sharks kill about ten humans per year; humans kill about one hundred million sharks per year. To give you some perspective, falling coconuts kill 150 people per year. But you'll never hear a conversation like this: "Honey, we need to get away, so I booked us a trip to Fiji next month!" And the response from their loved one is, "Fiji?! No way in hell I'm setting foot there. They have coconut trees." Sounds ridiculous, doesn't it? Well, it's not as ridiculous as being afraid of sharks, but people's beliefs, even if they're rooted in completely inaccurate belief systems, cause them to make decisions that have no basis in reality. This is what happens when we've been told something over and over again, year after year—even if something's not true, we believe it to be true.

Here's my disclaimer: What I'm about to share (and this pretty much goes for the entire book) are my thoughts and my thoughts only. What you're about to read isn't a popular opinion. Many in the personal growth world would wholeheartedly disagree with me because it would invalidate much of what they're forcing down our throats. And even crazier than having a contrarian and extremely unpopular opinion on the uselessness of goals is the fact that I believe goals cause more *harm* than good. I hope you're ready for this.

Do you know what percentage of people *hit* their goals? I'm talking about all people, all goals. Fitness, personal, business, financial, you name it. Take a guess.

Is it 75 percent, 50 percent, 33 percent? Try 8 percent![3] Depending on the study, and you can do the research yourself, between 5 percent and 20 percent of people hit their goals. Goals Calling's study reveals that 6 percent of people achieve their goals.[4] According to a University of Scranton study, 8 percent of people achieve their New Year's goals.[5]

Let that sink in. Less than one in ten people accomplish their goals. Surprised? I'm not. If roughly 90 percent of the adult population is not hitting their goals, how do you think they feel every day? Inspired? Motivated? Driven? Happy? Hell, no! Most of them feel disappointed, inadequate, incompetent, misaligned, or worse. Talk to any mental health professional—almost all of them will tell you these emotions don't lead to high performance. More importantly, if you're a sales manager and most of your salespeople spend every day dealing with these destructive emotions and negative thoughts, what would make you think that will lead to greater results and higher performance?

Before we dive into the idiocy of quotas, let's look at the approximately 8 percent of humans who actually hit their goals. In relation to sales, let's say a salesperson hits their goal or annual quota in September. What do you think most salespeople will naturally do? Yep, you guessed it; they slow down. This is a natural function of the human brain, and it's almost impossible to stop it. Take any salesperson you know who's way ahead of their quota, who's already achieved their bonus, earned their commission increase, or qualified for the company trip, and guess what most of them do? They coast. They ease up. They take their foot off the gas. We all know it.

How can this ever be considered a good thing? How many times have you seen this happen in the world of sports? A team gets up big. The game is seemingly over, and there's no way they can blow this lead. Then boom—momentum shifts. Fundamentals break down. Bad decisions are made. Opportunities are missed. You're now the Detroit Lions, who blew a 17-point lead over the 49ers in the 2023 NFC Championship. Or even worse, you're the Atlanta Falcons, who blew a 28–3 lead against the Patriots in the second half of Super Bowl LI.

Some people may disagree with my next point, which is par for the course of this book: Goals are clearly *not* the determining factor in championship performances. Let's use the Olympic Games for this example. Depending on the year, site, and season, one Olympic Games has roughly three hundred different events. Roughly ten thousand athletes from around the world compete in these events. They come from different cities, countries, and continents, and they all have unique family histories, backgrounds, physical characteristics, and coaches.

What's the goal of every one of those Olympic athletes? You know what it is. Every single one of them wants to win the gold medal. That has probably been their goal since they were either six years old or since they started dominating their sport in their teens. It's what they've been told they should strive for throughout their entire life up to this point.

Now, let's look at whether goals make the difference between gold medal winners and everyone else. Of the three hundred events taking place in a given Olympic Games, how many gold medals are given out? Yep, three hundred. And how many athletes had the same goal of winning the gold medal? Yep, probably all ten thousand. So, if all ten thousand had the same goal and only three hundred accomplished that goal, it's *not the goal that makes the difference!*

What makes the difference between gold medal winners and

everyone else? Well, it's not just one thing. It's a combination of many things, none of which include the goal. Here are some of the factors that drive gold medal–winning performances: preparation, effort, hard work, dedication, practice, mental toughness, facing adversity, sacrifice, more practice, eating habits, strength training, agility training, coaching, fundamentals, luck, genetics, timing, and execution. *Not goals!*

The athletes who perform to the best of their ability during a specific event will have the best chance to win a gold medal. Will they all? Nope. But if they stick to executing when they're on the track, field, or court, guess what will happen?

Here's another myth about goal setting: Your goals should be time-based. I'm not totally against thinking big and having dreams, but attributing a specific goal to a specific time frame, especially if it's more than a year away, is mind-boggling to me. If the average adult can't execute what they say they will do this weekend, what makes you think they can somehow execute some fantasy-filled wish that will supposedly take place over the next three, five, or ten years? It's insanity, if you ask me. The human brain is not designed to paint visions of a worry-free future and then easily lay out the yellow brick road we're supposed to follow to success. The human brain is the most powerful and most destructive organ we possess. As you're aware, when we don't follow through on what we say we're going to do (I'm sure you and I have never done such a thing), the negative self-talk kicks in, and we're doomed mentally for the next day, month, or even decade.

Unlike setting goals, writing to-do lists really works! We frequently use to-do lists to help us achieve our goals. You may use one; you may not. You may like them; you may hate them. Nevertheless, there are proven scientific, physiological, and psychological reasons why they're effective for most of the population. I'm sure you'll get differing opinions on this, and of course, you can find a study to prove or disprove just about any point someone could make. But to-do lists work because using them drives dopamine production in our brains, which triggers our brains to release the dopamine that tells us we're awesome.

Your brain tells you, "You rock! Great job! You did it! You're incredible!"

Negative self-talk is immensely destructive, but positive self-talk is incredibly uplifting. Which one do you think is better for salespeople, and which one do you think will lead to more sales? The crazy part is that by simply checking a box or crossing off a task on your to-do list, your brain tells you how amazing you are, and you'll be overwhelmingly more productive. And when your brain tells you how amazing you are, how does that make you feel? How do you think you'll feel the rest of the day? How will you show up to your family? Isn't that what life is all about?! Being happy?! This is why my favorite sales movie is *The Pursuit of Happyness*. And here's something the entire world of business needs to understand. Listen up.

Happy salespeople sell more stuff!!!

If it's true that happy salespeople sell more stuff, then why in the world would sales managers do everything in their power to ensure their salespeople are miserable?!

Let's go back to goals for a second, and then we'll address why assigning unrealistic quotas to salespeople defies logic, science, and common sense.

If 8 percent of people accomplish their goals, we can take that to mean 8 percent of salespeople accomplish their goals. We know the people who do accomplish their goals feel great every day, and their brains tell them they're awesome. Now, let's look at the flip side. If more than 90 percent of salespeople do not hit their goals, we know they'll feel disappointed, inadequate, incompetent, misaligned, and consider themselves failures. Their brains will be constantly telling them, "You're a loser. You're an idiot. You're a waste of space." Boy, that'll really inspire some self-confident, high-performing salespeople, won't it?

Quotas Are Dumb

Maybe we should start by defining the word dumb. You and I may have different definitions. When I say quotas are dumb, here's what I mean.

Quotas are nothing more than a fabricated goal based on some semblance of what may have happened in a prior time frame with a specific salesperson or sales team. Many people think I'm the dumb one for having this point of view, which is fine. But if you get a chance, ask salespeople if they are driven to sell more by the quotas arbitrarily assigned to them by people who've never set foot in the field. You'll only need to read their facial expression for the answer.

We'll come back to the stupidity of assigning arbitrary quotas in a minute, but first, let's discuss how quotas are created. Let's use a weather forecast as an example. You turn on the news to find out what the weather is going to be tomorrow. The meteorologist comes on and says, "We had a beautiful, eighty-one-degree day today, and I hope you all enjoyed some fun in the sun because we're in for a drastic change tomorrow. Unfortunately, it looks like it's going to be fifty-five degrees and rainy. I went and looked back at the weather we had last year on tomorrow's date, and it was fifty degrees and rainy." You would pause and ask yourself why they would need to look back to see what the weather was like on tomorrow's date of last year. That makes zero sense. What does the weather on May 3 of last year have to do with the weather on May 3 of this year?

You sit there, perplexed and flummoxed, trying to figure out the logic behind this forecast. The meteorologist comes back on screen and says, "Hey, everyone, I've done the research. I looked back to May 3 of last year—it was fifty degrees and rainy. So, with that knowledge, my forecast for tomorrow is fifty-five degrees and rainy. I calculated a 10 percent increase in temperature for no specific reason and with zero regard for logic and common sense."

WITAF? That stands for "What in the actual f**k?"

But that's exactly the logic behind how quotas are assigned!

For some inexplicable reason, salespeople are given a magic number to hit based on something that happened a year ago that has absolutely nothing to do with anything going on in today's selling environment. These imbecilic quotas are foisted on salespeople, and the people setting these quotas have almost no regard for what's happening *today*, in the now. Think back to one year ago from the day you're reading this. What has changed in the world? In your life? In your business? I'm going to go out on a limb here and say a hell of a lot has changed! Twelve months ago, salespeople may have

- had completely different products or services to sell,
- had completely different pricing models,
- had completely different sales cycles based on capacity,
- had completely different market conditions,
- had completely different supply chain challenges,

- been affected by completely different interest rates,
- had to execute completely different sales processes,
- had completely different contacts and buyers,
- built completely different relationships with clients, or
- had their champions leave the company.

Dozens of things could affect the amount of revenue salespeople generate from month to month, let alone from year to year. Yet, companies willingly and intentionally decide to ignore all of what I just shared and use some concocted BS percentage increase over the revenue generated last year. This is the quota that a salesperson is supposed to hit.

This unadulterated insanity is based on zero logic and no semblance of common sense, and it's still a standard practice in companies around the world! And if that's not bad enough, do you know what happens when a salesperson crushes their quota, breaks company sales records, earns a ton of commission, advances the company's brand, and generates their company a ton of profit?

They are *penalized*! Yep, you know it's true. They're penalized. *Not* rewarded. *Not* appreciated. *Not* thanked. *Not* valued. *They're penalized.* You've seen it. Hell, you may have even had it happen to you. I certainly have on multiple occasions.

Here's a real-life example that will make your blood boil. We had a client who would remain nameless. Their top salesperson was a woman named Yolanda. She was awesome. She was a go-getter, a driver, a powerhouse in sales, and an amazingly loyal employee. She was the number one salesperson on her team every year. After three consecutive years of crushing company records, her company decided to "alter" her compensation structure. She came to me for advice, and she was clearly distraught, disappointed, hurt, incredulous, and pissed off. I told her I would talk to the CEO and find out whether it was just a rumor or they were really considering doing something so insanely stupid.

I went to the CEO (we'll call him Todd) and said, "Todd, I heard through the grapevine you're considering changing Yolanda's compensation structure. Is this true?"

He said, "Steve, we can't have Yolanda making this kind of money. She's making too much."

I asked, "What do you mean she's making too much? If she sells $14M worth of equipment at a 15 percent gross margin, that means $2.1M in gross margin to your company, correct?"

Todd said, "Yes, that's right."

I said, "Okay, I'm fairly confident I understand basic math, and I know Yolanda made about $400K last year for bringing in $14M. Is that right?"

Todd nodded.

I asked, "Todd, what part of paying $400K and getting back $2.1M in gross margin is a bad thing for your business? Isn't she doing exactly what you'd want her to do as a salesperson?"

I'll never forget what Todd said next, and I promise you won't forget it, either. He said, "Steve, she's making more money than I am! We can't have a salesperson making more than her CEO."

I was stunned, shocked, and chagrined. I said to him, in not-so-subtle words, "Todd, let's get something straight. She's great, you're not."

They have yet to find a room in this country where Todd's ego could fit in, but when they do, I'll let you know. If I had stock in this company and I found out how he treats his salespeople and that he makes decisions for the company based on his fragile ego and weak-mindedness, I'd sell my stock instantly. When Yolanda told me they were planning to "alter" her compensation structure, she could already read the tea leaves. She gave her two weeks' notice before they officially penalized her and cut her pay for overperforming, and she immediately went to work for one of their direct competitors.

I'd like you to spend a few minutes thinking about this financial equation. The company wanted to cut Yolanda's pay by about $75K. Instead of paying their best, most incredible salesperson the money she deserved, here's what they lost:

- $14M a year in sales (if she continued to sell at that same pace)
- $2.1M a year in gross margin (if gross margins stayed at 15 percent)
- An amazing employee who always puts the company's needs before hers
- A great ambassador for their brand and a well-respected face of the company

I listed only a few of the things they lost—I'm sure you can imagine the list is a lot longer than that—but hey, at least they saved $75K. Even if her replacement could do 70 percent of what she could do, that idiotic decision cost that company at least $40M in top-line revenue and $6.3M in gross margin over ten years. The decision damaged their brand, strengthened their most direct competitor, and alienated their entire sales team. All to save $750K over ten years. Um, yeah. Good decision, Todd. But hey, we have to protect the CEO's ego, right?

Here's yet another reason quotas are monumentally idiotic. A quota is a made-up number. It's fairy dust. It's fantasy. It's created in some boardroom or on some Zoom call, and it's based on some formula, spreadsheet, CRM data, or historical performance. None of which has anything to do with what's happening *right now*.

More importantly, a quota is the company's goal, not the salesperson's. A quota is the private equity firm's goal, not the salesperson's goal. Take a minute and think about one of your neighbors. Just pick a name. Then, after you finish this chapter, walk over to their place, text them, or call them and ask for ten minutes of their time. Ask them to share all their goals and dreams for next year. Then, I want you to focus all your time, energy, effort, drive, and determination each day on accomplishing their goals. Does that sound exciting? Does it sound fun? Does it sound like something you can really put your heart and soul into? I don't think so.

Do sales managers and executives honestly think their salespeople go home at night, kiss their spouse good night, and say, "Honey, I don't know if I'm going to be able to sleep tonight. I'm so incredibly excited to wake up tomorrow and help our company improve its EBITDA! I can't wait!"

Let me fill you sales leaders in on a little secret from a salesperson's perspective. Most salespeople care about two entities in their lives: themselves and their families. That's it. And the best salespeople in the world have a third entity they care about—their clients. If salespeople are treated more like a number than human beings, and if they're looked at simply as a vessel for your company to achieve higher EBITDA (earnings before interest, taxes, depreciation, and amortization), they're not going to perform better! Yet, for some unknown reason, sales managers and executives think that pressuring their salespeople to hit some arbitrarily assigned, fabricated quota will somehow magically inspire unbelievable results. It's incomprehensibly dumb.

DPIs > KPIs

For those of you in sales leadership, the metrics you choose to focus on can hurt your sales team more than they help. Most businesses track KPIs (a.k.a. key performance indicators) to measure performance, track trends, analyze data, and forecast future results. The inherent problem is that most KPIs are lagging indicators—not all, but most. Measuring lagging indicators to determine future success is not a good idea. Measuring *leading* indicators is more effective and a better indicator of future success. What's the difference between lagging and leading indicators? A lagging indicator is something that is *caused* by an activity. For most businesses, that may include revenue, units sold, or customers acquired.

In baseball, the metric that determines which team wins the game is the number of runs scored. But the number of runs scored is a lagging indicator. If you want your team to win more games, you don't tell them, "Hey, team, score more runs!" In a sales context, it's like telling salespeople, "Sell more stuff!" Focusing on runs doesn't lead to more runs. You need to focus on consistently executing the activities that will lead to more runs. In baseball, you score more runs by getting more players on base. How do you get more players on base? You teach, coach, train, and help them execute more quality at bats. If they execute more quality at bats than the other team, that will lead to more players on base, which will lead to more runs, which will lead to more wins. In business, you can't simply tell your team to sell more and think that will drive more sales. You need your team to focus on the activities that will lead to more sales (quality at bats), and you've got to create systems and processes to ensure they're executing those activities consistently and with proficiency.

Let's walk through a deeper example in a baseball setting. (You don't need to understand baseball for this.) In baseball or softball, if you try your hardest to hit a home run, what usually happens? You strike out. We all know trying to hit home runs all the time is futile and will lead to much disappointment, fewer runs, and minimal success.

What's the goal when you go up to the plate in baseball or softball? Take a second to come up with your answer. Is it to get a hit? Is it to hit a home run? Is it to get on base? Nope. Stick with me, non-baseball fans. Is it possible to help your team win a game without physically making contact with the ball? The answer is yes—a resounding yes.

Here's the real goal when you go up to the plate in baseball or softball. It's to have a quality at bat. That could be a walk. It could be a sacrifice fly, it could be hitting the ball to the right side to move the runner over . . . it could be a lot of different things, none of which is getting a hit or a home run. The single best example of a player having a quality at bat is making the opposing pitcher throw a ton of pitches. Once again, stick with me, non-baseball fans!

A starting pitcher in baseball these days throws about eighty pitches in a game. When they approach pitch number eighty, they start getting tired, they become less effective, and they need to be pulled from the game. Let's say it's Game 7 of the World Series (the winner takes all), and my leadoff hitter (the first batter of a game) is up against Randy Johnson. This guy was one of the best pitchers of all time. He was six feet eleven inches tall and left-handed. He won five Cy Young awards, two World Series, and he killed a bird with a pitch! Seriously, look up "Randy Johnson kills bird" on YouTube right now.

Back to the analogy. Randy Johnson threw twenty-six pitches to the leadoff hitter, the first batter of Game 7. The batter isn't swinging at bad pitches—he's fouling off curve balls. He's not swinging at the high fastball—he's laying off the slider and making Randy Johnson work extremely hard to get him out. On the twenty-seventh pitch of the at bat, Randy Johnson finally strikes out the batter. How would you rate that at bat on a scale of one to ten, with ten being the best?

It's a twelve! Why is it a twelve, you ask?

Because the first batter of the game made Randy Johnson throw one-third of his total allotment of pitches (twenty-seven out of eighty) for an entire game to one batter. Therefore, Randy Johnson will be tired much earlier in the game than normal. He'll become less effective, he'll lose command of his pitches, he'll throw more balls than strikes, and he'll have to be replaced in the fifth inning rather than pitching the whole game. And if your team can avoid hitting against one of the greatest pitchers of all time and rather hit against pitchers of much lower quality, can you see how their chances of winning would increase dramatically?

The leadoff hitter did an amazing job tiring out Randy Johnson. Here's the most important part (stay with me here). After he strikes out on the twenty-seventh pitch, he walks back to the dugout where twenty-four other multimillionaire professional baseball players are waiting to greet him. What do these guys do when their teammate gets back to the dugout? Do they admonish him? Do they humiliate him? Do they chastise him? Do they emasculate him? Do they call him a loser? *No!* They high-five him! They pat him on the butt. They congratulate him.

Why on Earth would they recognize and appreciate someone who struck out and failed?! Because they know exactly how important that at bat was, and they know their entire team will benefit because they won't have to face Randy Johnson later in the game. They will get to face a weaker pitcher because of the efforts of that leadoff hitter. Now, even though he didn't get a hit, his "failure" makes it possible for the rest of his team to win Game 7 and the World Series.

Let's take a step back for one second and look again at lagging vs. leading indicators in a baseball context. If you didn't get to see the game and looked at the box score the next day (that's a list of all the stats from the game) and saw the leadoff hitter's *result* for that first at bat, what would show up in the box score?

A strikeout. The *result* of his at bat would be a strikeout.

And if you weren't familiar with baseball and were judging a player's success or failure based on a result (a hit, a home run, etc.), you'd look at the box score and call it a failure. During the game—and this is the funniest part—there are two diametrically opposed reactions people have to that strikeout. The first reaction is the one from his multimillionaire professional baseball–playing teammates, who are so excited, happy, and thankful he made Randy Johnson throw all those pitches, which is why they celebrate his effort, give him high-fives, etc. The other reaction comes from the idiot in the fifty-sixth row who couldn't hit a baseball to save his life. And after he watches the leadoff hitter strike out, this guy is screaming obscenities, giving him the middle finger, and telling his buddy he's an overpaid stiff.

Now, I ask you, which one of these people is the sales manager?

Is it the guy in the dugout who recognizes the true value of that strikeout and how much the team benefits from their leadoff hitter's failure?

Or is it the clueless fan in the stands who simply looks at meaningless statistics that have no real bearing on future success?

I think you know the answer.

Back to sales. What types of activities in sales would count for a quality at bat? To tie it all together, quality at bats in sales are what we call DPIs, or daily performance indicators. If baseball players consistently execute at bats with proficiency, they'll get on base more often. And if players get on base more often, the team will score more runs. And if the team scores more runs, they'll win more games! In a sales context, if salespeople execute their version of quality at bats consistently and with proficiency, known as DPIs, guess what magically increases? More opportunities. More opportunities lead to more meetings. More meetings lead to more proposals. More proposals lead to . . . more sales!

Not all DPIs are created equal, which means that not every salesperson in every company will have the same DPIs. Here's a list of some common DPIs that many salespeople focus on executing every day:

- Number of quality contacts made
- Number of lunches/dinners/coffee meetings scheduled
- Number of thank-you notes sent
- Number of LinkedIn and other posts published
- Number of client check-ins tallied
- Number of referrals requested
- Number of role-plays performed
- Number of minutes per day their craft was studied (fifteen)

Salespeople who focus on consistently executing four to six DPIs every day will ALWAYS generate more sales than salespeople who don't. The companies and leaders who drive and reward these activities will *always* generate more revenue than the companies that don't.

I'm not saying you should totally ignore KPIs and never track them again. Some companies' KPIs really are DPIs; they just don't call them the same thing. KPIs, in and of themselves, are pointless, like quotas. Activities drive KPIs and quotas, not the other way around. Ask a world-class personal trainer what they think is most important to track every day. Is it someone's weight, body fat percentage, and inches lost? Or is it tracking the number of miles they ran today, the number of pushups they did, and the number of calories they consumed? I think you know the answer. Having arbitrary KPIs and quotas like the number of deals closed, the amount of revenue generated this quarter, or any other misguided metrics will *not* drive more sales and revenue for you or your team. They will, however, drive significantly more stress, pressure, corner-cutting, sandbagging, and commission breath. What *will* drive more sales and revenue are the DPIs and daily tasks that salespeople complete every single day. And if they do them enough and do the right ones consistently every day, they'll make more sales.

The Daily 100

We just finished talking about the daily tasks that will ultimately drive your production and performance as a sales professional to higher levels. Now, let's discuss a very important process that can be life-changing for you and your sales career. As we all know, the sales landscape is always evolving. Our team is constantly exploring new methodologies and strategies to drive performance, engagement, and productivity for our clients.

One such methodology that we see best-in-class organizations adopting is gamification. Why is gamification crucial in sales? Because selling is a performance-driven activity. Just like in games, we have targets, scores, competition, and rewards. When we inject the fun and engaging elements of games into sales, we tap into an innate desire for achievement, competition, and recognition. This leads to heightened engagement, motivation, and overall performance.

There is one tool we use to help our clients implement gamification into their sales organizations. It's called the Daily 100, which was born from decades of studying salespeople and identifying the most important activities that ultimately lead to success. Driving daily activity is more important than any other aspect of professional selling. Give me a salesperson who's a badass when it comes to daily activity over a salesperson who's got an amazing skill set any day of the week. The Daily 100 is a guideline for completing specific DPIs that will increase your activity and cause your performance and results to increase.

The Daily 100 is a daily checklist of the tasks and duties you need to accomplish every day, regardless of the outcomes. You're given points based on the number and types of activities you complete. For example, a new dial or contact is worth one point, whereas a meeting with the ultimate decision-maker is worth thirty points. And I can promise you this. If you increase your activity, you'll increase your sales. Not maybe. Not probably. Always, 100 percent of the time. You already know the results you've been getting without using a Daily 100. Now, let's see the results you can create in the next ninety days if you do the Daily 100, every day, for ninety days in a row.

DETACHING FROM OUTCOMES

"IT'S A BOLD STRATEGY, COTTON. Let's see if it pays off for 'em."[1] These may be funny words of wisdom (uttered by Pepper Brooks in the movie *Dodgeball*), but I'm dead serious. I've embraced, internalized, and lived this mantra, strategy, or modus vivendi (way of living) for the past few years, and it has completely changed my life. My worldview is entirely different from what it was early in my career, and detaching from outcomes has led to enormous positive and life-altering effects. Letting go is unnatural for me or almost any other human being, but the next mantra clearly spells out the need to do so. We've all heard of Abraham Maslow's Hierarchy of Needs, which is still relevant today. However, a much more poignant idea about detachment has been attributed to Maslow: "The only way to truly be happy is to be free from any outcomes."

An outcome is the endpoint or culmination of a series of actions or events and often reflects the success or failure of that specific endeavor. Outcomes can be tangible or intangible and encompass a wide range of possibilities, including achievements, consequences, goals, or effects that result from one's efforts or circumstances. These results can be measured and evaluated, and they may significantly impact an individual's life, well-being, or satisfaction.

My interpretation of what Maslow said is that happiness comes from detaching from results because you cannot control results. Nobody can! You may think you can, but you cannot. You can only control yourself, your actions, your words, your thoughts, your activities, and your mindset. Unequivocally, you cannot control the results of your actions, no matter how hard you try. The fact that most people worry about what's outside of their control is the issue. When it comes to sales, the ability to detach from the outcome is the polar opposite of what we've been taught for decades. I know it sounds weird, but if you can find happiness, contentment, and fulfillment in the process or journey itself, rather than basing your existence solely on achieving specific results or quotas, you'll be more successful. And by taking the focus off selling, you'll sell more!

Listen up, sales managers! Salespeople have more value in this life than becoming a mule to carry your company's water down the Grand Canyon of EBITDA. They have families, friends, passions, hobbies, personal responsibilities, and many more reasons for living besides dedicating 100 percent of their waking hours to driving revenue for your organization. That's the straight-up truth.

Let's talk about the outcomes that are constantly forced down salespeople's throats, all of which they could never control in a million years:

- Number of appointments
- Monthly, quarterly, or annual targets (a.k.a. quotas)
- Revenue goals
- Sales—all sales, forever and ever, from now until the end of time

For the life of me, I still don't know when all this stuff started, but it's causing the opposite effect that companies want from their sales teams. Let's briefly address each outcome.

Setting appointments in the traditional manner (a salesperson calling by phone, let's say) involves two parties: the dialer and the receiver of the call. The last time I checked, a salesperson making calls can't control whether someone picks up the phone. If that's the case, and it is the case one hundred out of one hundred times, why should a salesperson be judged on the number of appointments they set? It makes no sense. They didn't have any opportunities to set any appointments. Now, if they dialed one hundred times, physically spoke to fourteen ideal decision-makers, and set zero appointments, then we can narrow down where the problem lies. But if a salesperson dials one hundred times, doesn't speak to one ideal decision-maker, and sets zero appointments, they're made to feel like a loser—despite having done nothing wrong.

As we discussed already, quotas are dumb. They are nothing more than a fabricated number that's based on some semblance of what may have happened in a prior time frame with a specific salesperson or sales team. Quotas would only make sense if your business had a finite existence, such as a single summer season. I'm assuming, though—and maybe I shouldn't—that you plan on being in business longer than next month, next quarter, or next year. And if your company plans on being around for a long time, what conceivable reason would exist for assigning magic numbers to an unending calendar of days, weeks, and months? Will the currency you receive lose its monetary value if it's received on the second day of the following month? Do you really think forcing your salespeople to jam your product or service down the throats of prospects who are not ready, just to achieve a magic number created in a boardroom, will lead to you accumulating more of your coveted revenue? I think not.

Targeting a made-up revenue goal that is based on made-up math and outdated data from last year's performance lacks any semblance of logic or common sense. You can use examples from any aspect of life, and it simply doesn't equate. Could you possibly and accurately predict your child's score on their fourth-grade math quiz tomorrow by looking back to last year's third-grade math quiz on the same date? Of course not! If you're a golfer, could you possibly and accurately predict the score you'll shoot at Pebble Beach on May 3 next week by looking back to the score you shot at St. Andrews last May 3? Hell no!

Sales are the one thing that sales managers believe to be in the hands of their salespeople, but sales are not remotely in their hands, and they never will be. Ever. I know many sales leaders who would love it if their salespeople could secretly hack into their prospects' bank accounts and wire the money directly into their accounts; fortunately for buyers, it doesn't quite work like that. Buyers are the ones who decide whether they're going to buy or not. Let me make this crystal clear—*buyers* decide whether they're going to buy. As a salesperson, you can certainly help them make an educated decision on whether to buy from you or not, but you cannot ever choose for them. And if that's the case, why would salespeople be punished for something they have zero control over?

You can make a colossal difference if you're one of the few sales-people and even fewer organizations who've embraced this concept of detachment. We have a client in an extremely important and well-known industry who has never, I repeat, *never*, had revenue goals, quotas, or outcome-based targets. To share some stats, their company

- has been in business for twenty years;
- achieves 10 percent to 20 percent growth, year over year, every year they've been in existence;
- has an average salesperson tenure of twelve years (US company average is eighteen months);
- has Net Promoter Scores in the high nineties;
- has customer satisfaction scores in the high nineties;
- has less than 5 percent annual turnover among all employees; and
- expects to break $200M in revenue next year.

Guess what they *did not* have for goals! They did not plan to

- grow at least 10 percent per year;
- shoot for a salesperson tenure of at least twelve years;
- have 95 percent+ Net Promoter Scores;
- have 98 percent+ customer satisfaction scores;
- have less than 5 percent annual turnover; or
- break $200M by their twentieth year.

They accomplished all those incredible things, but they didn't write them down as goals, they didn't stencil their targets on the wall in the conference room, they didn't shove those goals down their salespeople's throats, and they didn't forecast a magical path to success guided by spreadsheet jockeys. Here's exactly what they do every day. They

- focus on making their customers' lives easier;

- innovate and improve upon what may already be working well;

- take care of their employees as if they're immediate family, and

- invest in their sales and leadership team more than they think they need.

They have done several other things to achieve phenomenal success, but this list is a good start. I know the heads of some of my readers have now exploded, and brain matter is strewn across this page, but that's not surprising, given the business world we live in today.

When you're attached to outcomes—meaning you derive self-esteem from someone else's actions—you will end up doing whatever it takes to get the outcome your ego says is right for you, even when the realistic situation calls for something different. This is precisely why the revenue-first executive teams and the ABC fools are hindering their revenue growth, not increasing it.

The incomparable Jim Rohn has an amazing take on the subject of detachment. He said, "It's not what happens that determines your life's future. It's what you do about what happens."[2] And what that really means to me is this: Do what you can, learn all you can, create a presence in the marketplace, execute your DPIs every day, and the outcome will be the outcome. Be willing to embrace whatever happens. You can't control it anyway.

Why Can't Most People Detach?

Whether you're a sales leader or salesperson, detachment is a difficult concept to embrace. We get attached to whether we get to work on time.

We get attached to whether we set an appointment with a prospect. We get attached to whether the prospect will buy something from us. We even get attached to the goals other people have for us, and we're not in control of that one bit! (Reason #29 why quotas are dumb.)

I think the reason most people can't grasp the concept of detachment is because of the way they were raised (including me). Depending on your generation, your thoughts about chasing results and outcomes may vary significantly. An individual's tendency to obsessively chase results is born from various psychological factors and childhood experiences. The following are just some of the reasons that may have led people to this worldview.

Conditional Love or Need for Approval

Growing up in an environment where love, attention, or approval is conditional on achievements can develop the belief that a person is only worthy or lovable when they succeed. In Chapter 7, I explain how detrimental a salesperson's need to be liked can be; that need is part of some salespeople's Sales DNA.

High or Unrealistic Expectations

Some parents may place extremely high expectations on their children, leading them to internalize a belief that they must always perform at a top level to be considered good enough. You know exactly who I'm talking about. These are the whacked-out pageant moms living vicariously through their daughters or the hot-headed, maniacal sports dads who scream at coaches and umpires at Little League games. These people have unresolved issues, and they have no idea what kind of trauma they're causing their children.

Modeling Behavior

As we all know, kids often reflect the behavior of their parents. If their parents or other influential adults in their lives modeled behavior that was overly focused on results and outcomes, those kids will focus on results and outcomes as well. In the late '80s, there was an after-school special TV commercial where a teenage boy gets caught smoking pot by his dad, and his father says to him angrily, "Who taught you how to do this stuff?" The boy replies, "You, all right! I learned it by watching you."[3]

Perfectionism

Growing up in a highly competitive environment, whether academically, athletically, or otherwise, a child will often learn that their value is tied to their ability to outperform others in pursuit of perfection. If perfection was expected or there was an extreme aversion to mistakes, a child may develop perfectionist tendencies, making it really hard for them to detach from the desire for flawless results. This trauma is hard to overcome.

Focusing on Results Doesn't Help

Many incredible authors, thought leaders, world-renowned psychologists, medical professionals, and global icons have thoughts on detachment. Deepak Chopra highlights this point wonderfully in his book *Seven Spiritual Laws of Success*, in which he writes:

> In order to acquire anything in the physical universe—you must relinquish your attachment to it. It does not mean you give up the intention to create your desire. You don't give up the intention. You give up your attachment to the results. Attachment is based on fear and insecurity. And the need for security is based on not knowing one's true self.[4]

Henry David Thoreau wrote, "The mass of men lead lives of quiet desperation,"[5] which is a metaphor for desperate attachment. I could include many more quotes and examples, but I don't want to belabor the point.

Most salespeople are paid based on results, reinforcing and solidifying their attachment to outcomes. If you're told by your sales manager that you need to hit your numbers or else *or* that your bonus is tied to how much revenue you produce this quarter, you'll start to focus on whatever it takes to accomplish that. This is not the best way to drive sales. If revenue is the goal you're attached to fulfilling, you'll do whatever it takes to hit that goal, which isn't always a good thing. You'll take on bad clients who are late making payments, don't follow the directions you gave them, refuse to return calls promptly, and create a plethora of other stress-inducing situations that will make you wish you had never met them. We all have those clients. Sometimes, we wish they had never been born; that's how bad it is. And if that's the case, why did you take them on as a client in the first place?! All the signs were there, all the red flags were apparent, and you ignored them all in the pursuit of revenue.

Salespeople and sales managers always seem to assume that hearing the word *yes* is the ultimate goal and proof of success. In reality, the best thing you can do when you sense a potentially problematic client is to say *no*. You can easily avoid disaster by not taking on a problem client, saving you from wasting your time fixing issues you shouldn't have to fix, adding stress to your day, and receiving negative reviews because the client is never happy. Instead of taking on problem clients solely because you "need" the revenue, when you say NO, you can focus your time on more ideal clients, more profitable deals, more enjoyable experiences, and stronger relationships, which will always lead to happier customers, more referrals to people just like them, and more profitable and repeat business.

I get it. I know this is a stretch for some salespeople who are reading this right now. But when you're detached from the outcome of a sale, you'll sell more stuff. Detachment leads to *greater outcomes*, especially in sales. When you're unconcerned with whether a prospect will buy and you're not spewing commission breath all over them, they're more likely to buy. If you pull up to the car dealership and the car salespeople look at you like seagulls eyeing up a french fry at the beach, you're less likely to buy a car.

In the B2B world, when a prospect says they need to think about it or run it past legal, here's the answer you give: "No problem." In the B2C world, when a prospect says they need to talk to their spouse, here's the answer you give: "No problem."

But that's not what 99 percent of salespeople have been taught. They've been taught old-school, antiquated, mindless objection-handling techniques like the good ole "feel, felt, found" garbage or any of the other unending number of abhorrently idiotic closing tricks.

Here's why detachment works. Let's say you have ten prospects, two of whom will buy, two will never buy, and six may buy at some point.

The ABC zealots will try to close all eight prospects (the two ready to buy plus the six who may buy at some point) at any cost. In doing so, they have now alienated eight potential future buyers, driven them into the hands of the competition, left a bad taste in their mouths, perpetuated the myth that all salespeople are slimeballs, damaged their company's name and brand in the process, and solidified the prospects' resolve to never buy from their company. But alas, they held one of the prospects hostage until they said yes, forced them to buy when they weren't ready, and set the groundwork for buyer's remorse a month from now. But hey, congratulations, they hit their monthly quota! Woohoo! They made their commission, and in praise, their manager puts their name on the leaderboard and uses them as an example of someone who comes through when the company needs them to.

I hope you can hear the sarcasm dripping from my words. And if you can't, please absorb what I'm telling you and realize that this is exactly how most companies want their salespeople to behave. And even worse, if you're a sales manager, your colleagues applaud, encourage, and expect this exact behavior from their salespeople, as if this is somehow a good thing. Please, someone, wake me from this nightmare.

Let's look at that same example again, but this time, let's see what might happen if you act like a normal human being and not an outcome-driven robot. Take the same ten prospects: two will buy (from anyone), two will never buy, and six may buy at some point. All six potential buyers will have some level of concern, objection, fear, uncertainty, lack of information, or any number of other things preventing them from buying today. So, instead of being the traditional ABC salesperson, you detach from the outcome (the sale), and you simply say, "No problem." Even if you think that's foolish, six prospects will leave that meeting in a better mood. They will leave that meeting surprised, stunned, and maybe even a little relieved that you didn't treat them like your next mark, the next notch on your belt, or the next metric kicker to your quarterly bonus. In turn, you've annoyed none of them, you've kept the door open for future business, and you've shown them their business means something to you, whenever and whether that moment ever arrives.

But according to some sales managers, you're a loser. You didn't hit your monthly quota. You'll be humiliated in front of the rest of the team, and you may even be put on a performance improvement plan (PIP). Who cares about the two prospects out of the six who come back later to tell you how thankful they were that you didn't push them and pay for your services in full because now's the time they really need them? They write an amazing five-star review online, give you a glowing LinkedIn recommendation, and personally refer you to three more clients, who in turn refer you to their colleagues, which leads to another $10M in revenue. Who wants that, anyway?

Detaching from outcomes is a form of strength, not a sign of weakness. It will attract more people to you at a higher psychological and emotional level, especially clients. When you enter a sales conversation with a prospect, and they can see you don't care whether they buy or not, more of them will consider you a trusted advisor and not a street peddler pushing three-card monte on them. More clients will want to buy from you, more of those clients will refer others who want to buy from you, and you'll generate more sales because you're not focused on generating more sales!

The Oxymoronic Effects of Chasing Results

When you embrace the power of detaching from outcomes, your results will *increase*. You will focus on the present moment and perform at your best without being distracted by the fear of failure or the pressure to succeed. This concept—negative results caused by focusing on outcomes—applies to many different aspects of life.

Dating

Aggressively pursuing someone (up to and including stalking them) will usually push them away. Overeagerness can come off as desperation or lacking self-worth, which isn't attractive. "I texted you eight times! Why haven't you responded?"

Sports

In baseball, if you swing as hard as you can to hit a home run, you'll strike out. In golf, if you swing as hard as you can to hit the ball three hundred yards, well, let's just say it won't go three hundred yards.

Nature

If you chase an animal, it's likely to run away. But if you sit there and wait quietly and patiently, the animal may come to you.

Meditation

Trying too hard to clear your mind will do the opposite and make your head spin even more.

Fitness

Overtraining and lifting weights that are too heavy for you will cause more injuries and decrease your performance and results.

Sales

If you're an ABC robot who deploys high-pressure sales tactics and arm-wrestles people into buying from you, you'll sell less. "Patience is a virtue." Ever heard that phrase before? It's true.

The Four Benefits of Detachment

If you can somehow muster up the strength, courage, and commitment to detach from outcomes, you might experience the following four life-altering benefits.

One: Increased Focus

Detaching from outcomes will help you focus on the present moment and the task at hand rather than worrying about what may or may not happen in the future. Focus on what you need to execute *right now*, not in an hour, not tomorrow, and certainly not by the end of the quarter. Today, as in *this moment right now*, is all you can control.

Two: Increased Creativity and Innovation

When you detach from outcomes, you are free to explore unique possibilities and ideas outside the box without being limited by the fear of failure. This will help you generate new ideas and more innovative solutions to problems that seem unsolvable. You might explore possibilities you had never considered before.

Three: Stronger Resilience

Detaching from outcomes can help you bounce back more quickly from setbacks or failures because you're not defined by a specific result. This can help you stay on track and focus on the task at hand, even in the face of challenges.

Four: Reduced Stress and Anxiety

When you are overly attached to a specific outcome, you'll typically experience heightened levels of stress and anxiety, which can negatively impact your performance. By detaching from outcomes, you will reduce your stress levels substantially and perform better as a result. Pressure doesn't increase performance in most people, especially not in salespeople!

Let me be absolutely clear. Detaching from outcomes doesn't mean you're flippant. It doesn't mean you're carefree, lazy, or unmotivated. It doesn't mean you don't want to hit your numbers, achieve your quota, or make a great income. It means you're okay with whatever happens.

A great exercise to try is to reflect on the last thirty days and note each situation in which you felt that attachment to an outcome negatively affected you. You may want to do this with your sales leader or a colleague because when you're emotionally involved in a process, it's not always easy to see the negative effects on yourself. As you look back and view things now (hindsight is 20/20), really dissect your actions and behaviors and recall the emotions you felt and exhibited along the way during that deal. You can also take a deeper dive into how you communicated with your prospect throughout the sales process to see how your attachment to outcomes impacted the result. Were you too aggressive? Did you listen attentively? Did you miss an important detail? Did you act in your own best interest? Did you push them to buy too soon? Did you follow up with their needs or your own needs in mind?

By detaching from outcomes, you'll be happier, you'll perform better, you'll be more creative, people will want to spend more time with you, and you will achieve greater success in your personal and professional life.

(3)

BEWARE THE FAKE GURUS

WHETHER YOU'RE A SALESPERSON, a sales leader, an owner, or a CEO, you probably agree that increasing sales and driving new revenue are critical components of business. The challenge is that many companies don't know exactly how to accomplish those two things in the best way possible. So, they look for shortcuts, microwave results, magic funnels, fool-proof lead-gen consultants, or any other flavor of the month who promises endless amounts of revenue for the low, low price of $997. An unending line of fake gurus is constantly coming out of the woodwork like termites. These frauds have all teamed up with one another to create the illusion of success through social media, fake social proof, and wild claims that are somehow legally protected because of their disclaimers that say, "Results are not typical." These charlatans wouldn't make it one hour if they had to cut their teeth in professional selling, which is why they relentlessly market to the naïve, desperate, and downtrodden people who want instant results without putting in the work. The world of multilevel marketing is full of the same BS, promising endless riches, financial freedom, and carefree lifestyles brimming with Italian sports cars, fancy watches, trophy spouses, and, of course, passive income. Same s**t, different day.

Unfortunately, these scams have thrived for decades with no real system of checks and balances, and because they all have disclaimers, they have a license to ruin people's lives and destroy their families. I wish I were joking. Real estate schemes, protein shakes, drop shipping, and non-fungible tokens (NFTs) are just a few entries from a long list of can't-miss business opportunities. I remember one TV ad from the '90s by a guy named Don Lapre. His trademark sales pitch was this: "By placing tiny classified ads in newspapers, I'm able to make $50,000 a week from my tiny one-bedroom apartment."[1] You can look this up; it's real and has quite a sad ending. Don Lapre was charged with forty-one counts of conspiracy, mail fraud, wire fraud, and promotional money laundering. According to Dahyi Shira's article in *People*, Lapre "allegedly scammed more than $50M from at least 220,000 people.... Two days before he was to stand trial ... Lapre was found dead in his Arizona jail cell—an apparent suicide."

The most recent example of these fake gurus comes from a movie featuring Leonardo DiCaprio, in which he portrays a drug-fueled stockbroker slinging penny stocks to steal more than $200M from unsuspecting investors. Do you know some companies have hired this convicted felon? They hired this criminal—who still hasn't made his court-mandated restitution payments and who knowingly ruined the lives of hundreds of people (most of whom will never recover)—to teach their team how to sell! Are you kidding me?!

If you have been on social media for the last ten years, the next fake guru I discuss is the self-proclaimed uncle of the soulless, emotionless, and unscrupulous people who treat money as if it somehow bestows immortality. (Funny, I almost typed immorality, which is also appropriate.) He is a self-proclaimed real estate billionaire (he's not really a billionaire) who claims he will magically change your life. In reality, he has hoodwinked you into thinking he's an expert in a field you know very little about. This is the formula for the fake guru. Spend tens of millions on social media by creating a persona feigning wisdom and affecting expertise in a field they knew nothing about five years ago.

There's another repulsive fake guru who berates people if they don't have six-pack abs. For real, I'm not kidding. Besides the fact he's probably on the juice, he claims that if you don't have washboard abs, you clearly don't care about your success in life, and you'll never make it.

The list of these frauds is endless, and I wish I could name all these vile human beings so you know who to avoid at all costs. But I'm sure one of their brainwashed lemmings would probably sue me, so I'll leave their names out of this book. You may already know whom I'm referring to, and if you don't, they're quite easy to find on social media, targeting the naïve with their daily grift.

I hope it's not the case, but you may have gone through some of these fake gurus' online courses, participated in their overpriced and valueless masterminds, or attended a stadium event full of personal-growth zombies looking for their next fix. If you did, I'm so sorry. For the overwhelming majority of people, these schemes don't work. They never have, and they never will. Do you think Jeff Bezos, Sara Blakely, Carlos Slim, Rihanna, or any other successful businessperson achieved success because they learned a secret selling method? Or because they paid $50K for a mastermind or learned how to be a closer? Yeah, that must be it. Or maybe it was attending a weekend event where they learned a magic funnel . . . that's got to be it!

Let's take a minute to address why microwaving your business and personal growth doesn't work. There is literally no part of life or business that can be dramatically improved over the weekend. In forty-eight hours, here are some of the things you CAN'T do:

- Learn a language.
- Master a musical instrument.
- Become a scratch golfer.
- Graduate from college.
- Lose twenty-five pounds.
- Win the Nobel Prize.

However, according to these frauds, here's what you can accomplish over the weekend:

- Become a real estate investor.
- Become an Amazon drop shipper.
- Become an affiliate marketer.
- Become a business coach.
- Become a social media expert.
- Become a world-class closer.

The list continues, but I have to finish writing this book, so I'll stop at those six empty promises by the fake gurus. Can you imagine if all it took to become a physician was $5K and attendance over the weekend to be able to care for, diagnose, treat, and operate on human bodies? How confident would you be going to a hospital full of surgeons who learned in this way? What if the requirements to becoming an airline pilot amounted to a $497 offer (but it's really worth $49,997!) that gained your admittance into a Facebook group run by a twenty-two-year-old who still struggles to shave properly but does, however, have all the answers to the meaning of life? Or better yet, what if master's degrees could be obtained by signing up through an Instagram sales funnel?

And last, I'll mention the whole magic funnel garbage that's endlessly promoted on social media. These magic funnels are all you need to leave your corporate nine-to-five, work from home, and make $50K/month. It's easy! You can achieve endless amounts of passive income with no training, no money, no skill, no talent, no product, no ability, and no effort. All for only $497!

Sounds legit, doesn't it?

Do yourself a favor and look up Mike Winnett. He created something a few years ago called the Contrepreneur Formula and Contrepreneur Bingo, and they are hilarious.[2] He calls out these frauds and fake gurus and shows you the system they follow to separate the naïve and downtrodden from the money in their bank accounts. Worst of all, unfortunately, are the self-proclaimed sales "experts." These scammers are so repulsive and repugnant that merely the thought of having them speak with my clients, colleagues, friends, or family makes my skin crawl.

The time has come to encourage your friends, families, colleagues, and fellow sales professionals to stop giving these relentless grifters your money. Most of these frauds wouldn't last two minutes in the real business world, which is why they can only thrive in the world of social media. They know their target audience and hunt them down like lions stalking wounded gazelles. These charlatans are all selling to the same people, who continue to buy all their garbage, thinking the next special offer will take them to another level. It won't.

"Magic" Selling Systems Don't Work

Now that I've warned you to beware of the fake gurus and the dreck they peddle, let's dive a bit more into the systems of selling that are promoted by the people who pitch endless riches. Selling has been relatively easy for the last decade. From about 2011 to 2019, things were easy. The economy was humming, businesses were thriving, and consumers were spending lots of money. Housing boomed, technology expanded, and discretionary income was high. All those factors added up to perfect conditions for salespeople. Most of them sat back, relaxed, and took orders. Then came 2020, and the pandemic bumped people's sales numbers even higher, along with their perceived value to the marketplace, and everyone watched the revenue roll in.

News flash! Things have changed. With the economic climate we're in today, and probably for the next few years, if you don't transform, recalibrate, and learn how to sell to today's consumers in this unique marketplace, you're going to be left in the dust. That's why old-school, manipulative tactics based on building rapport, reciting scripts, and following outdated "magic" selling systems don't work anymore.

The list of magic selling systems that have been peddled for decades is endless, but I won't list the names here. You can look them up if you want to. One antiquated technique that's still taught today is called the upfront contract. Another uses a four-letter acronym for a regurgitated style of questioning and claims that prospects are defenseless against your charm if you use this method. In addition, they promote stuttering on purpose to pretend like you're confused when talking to a prospect, combined with shuffling meaningless papers around to create a sound as if you're shuffling through important documents. Yes, I'm not lying. And these phony and fake techniques are somehow going to flip a switch in their brain and make them want to buy from you.

I'm here to tell you—and I'm sorry to burst your bubble—that there is no one-size-fits-all system of selling. Imagine a world where there's only one car manufacturer with one model of car to buy. Or a world where there's only one golf club manufacturer with one exact way to swing the club. Or a world with only one restaurant chain that serves only one meal to all its customers.

Let's expand on that for a moment. Let's say the restaurant only serves boiled chicken. This is precisely what a magic selling system preaches: You, the salesperson, need to serve boiled chicken to everyone. But there are hundreds of ways to cook chicken, and if you want to please customers, have them come back again and again, and, you know, pay for the type of meal they choose, you may want to cook it the way they like it. Just a thought.

This is why teaching one-size-fits-all magic selling systems defies logic. The most effective salespeople will master their *own* techniques. They'll build muscle memory, confidence, and habits that allow them to specifically tailor the sales process to the person they're selling to. That includes learning market conditions, unique selling situations, a prospect's individual buying behaviors, and numerous other factors. Pretending there is one magic selling system, one magic questioning technique, one magic closing question, or one magic method of manipulation that convinces all your prospects to buy from you is laughable.

Can you imagine a world where your business charges the same prices for your product or service that it charged in 1950, when bread was fourteen cents, cars were $1,300, and homes were $7,500? That's precisely what's been happening for decades in the sales training space! Obviously, this is a bit tongue-in-cheek, but I'm dead serious. Much of what's still being taught in sales training stems from the 1950s, and only minuscule slivers of it are still applicable today. The "feel, felt, found" method, trial closes, and "yes ladders" are only a few of the outdated, obsolete, and ineffective techniques that are still peddled today by sales training companies and several fake gurus. The world of business has changed astronomically in the past few years, let alone in the past seventy years. If business, prices, language, culture, technology, processes, software, employment, income, strategy, tools, and industries have all changed dramatically, why wouldn't people think that the way we sell also needs to change?

Why the Next Generation Doesn't Want to Enter the World of Sales

It's not like the young people of previous generations *wanted* to go into sales, and today's younger generations don't exactly have "sales professional" at the top of their list of desired vocations. Can you blame them?! Why do young people have little interest in joining this amazing profession? Probably because the perception of salespeople is terrible! It always has been, and it always will be. Salespeople are looked upon as the dregs of society (I'm being polite here). In Daniel Pink's book *To Sell Is Human*, he asked several thousand people the first word that came to mind when they heard "sales" or "selling." The following word cloud shows their top twenty responses.

The most commonly chosen word was *pushy*! *Yuck* was the second most common word. Yuck! Here's the actual word cloud from the study for your amusement.

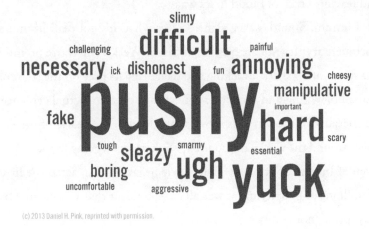

(c) 2013 Daniel H. Pink, reprinted with permission.

Figure 3.1. Copyright © 2013 Daniel H. Pink. Reprinted with permission from *To Sell Is Human: The Surprising Truth About Moving Others.*

After reading *To Sell Is Human* and several recent articles about this topic, I realized that my passion for changing the perception of salespeople is needed now more than ever. The demand for great salespeople has never been higher, and thanks to the leaders in corporate America who feel that laying off their workforce is a strategy for growth, many incredibly talented women and men are looking for a new place to land.

The movie *Jaws* taught me a lot about sales. We all know the bone-chilling, two-syllable sound that still strikes fear into the hearts of millions, even five decades later: Duh-duh. Duh-duh. Duh-duh. It's a story about a rogue thirty-foot-long great white shark that unleashes utter chaos and horror on a quaint little beach town on Amity Island. The island's inhabitants eagerly anticipate the Fourth of July holiday, and they are preparing for their annual celebration and associated influx of tourists. Little do they know, they're in for the shock of their lives as a voracious predator starts killing unsuspecting beachgoers and leaving a trail of blood in its wake.

Hmmm. Sounds scary, right? Guess what. It's not real! It's not a documentary! It's not an episode of Shark Week! The entire premise of a man-eating shark attacking and devouring its prey off the coast of a small New England vacation spot is based on zero factual evidence. But because of the fear this movie embedded in the hearts of movie-goers around the world, millions of people stopped going in the water! Even in Indiana! Seriously. That movie negatively impacted the lives of millions of people, and it was all based on fear that was created by perception, not reality.

This is what *Jaws* taught me about sales: Perception is reality. Whether it's based on fact or not, people will believe things that could be 100 percent false because of their perceptions. And what's the general perception of salespeople? Rude, aggressive, pushy, obnoxious, arrogant, heartless, and a whole list of other unflattering adjectives and characteristics. Why do you think people think so negatively of salespeople? It is because of the way salespeople have been taught to sell for decades. Salespeople have been taught to take no prisoners when it comes to sales. Push-push-push, close-close-close. Don't take no for an answer. We've all been subjected to these high-pressure techniques a million times while buying a car, furniture, solar, software, uniforms, CRMs, and many other products and services. This is the way sales-people have been taught, and as consumers, the way we assume they will act. When most salespeople open their mouths, we think they're slimy because they lead us to believe they *are* a slimy salesperson. And that's what *Jaws* taught me. When the average person sees a shark, they freak out. Why? Because of the perception that it's going to eat them. It's conditioning, it's preemptive, it's ingrained, and even though it's wrong 99 percent of the time, we don't care. "That shark is going to kill me, so therefore, I'll never go swimming again!" To sum this up, if you're in sales or if you're a sales leader, and your salespeople talk, text, email, write, converse, follow up, speak, and behave like 99 percent of other salespeople, your prospects assume they're going to be hoodwinked, sold, or closed.

This is precisely why we must change the way we sell in today's marketplace. I recommend reviewing your entire sales process from top to bottom to ensure your salespeople aren't making their prospects feel like they're stalked by a great white shark. You must examine the way they prospect, conduct demos, follow up, write emails, send requests for proposals (RFPs), present to groups, nurture clients, ask for the business, and all other aspects of their role as salespeople to ensure they do not sound like salespeople.

Always Be Helping (*Not* Always Be Closing)

Always be helping. It just sounds good. It sure as hell sounds better than always be closing. Closing is for bad salespeople. World-class sales professionals do not close. Instead, their prospects ask them how to move forward.

"What's the next step, Darnell?"

"When do we get started?"

"How do we begin?"

Those are the questions that world-class sales professionals hear from their prospects. Please, I'm begging you, for the love of all you consider holy, stop arm-wrestling your prospects into buying. Stop forcing people to buy your solution when they're clearly not ready to buy. It's idiotic, and it lessens the chances of you making a sale in the long run. Closing is an old-school, antiquated pile of dog crap that continues to exacerbate the perception that salespeople are pushy and only care about one thing—getting your money. I'm begging you to stop, on behalf of all human beings.

The perpetuation of the stereotype of the slimy salesperson is continuously promoted through ridiculous Hollywood interpretations of what salespeople act like, as I shared earlier. When drug-fueled felons and fake stock–selling swindlers are glorified by Hollywood, and the lifestyle of stealing money is promoted as glamorous and rewarding, what other perceptions could people draw about salespeople?

When we think about the term *closing*, we automatically think of ABC, right? It's been ingrained in your mind if you've been in sales for a significant period. By this point, you know it comes from the movie *Glengarry Glen Ross*, which I describe in Chapter 1. The company's top salesman, Blake, is a perfect example of an unethical, immoral, and greedy salesperson who uses high pressure and coercion to browbeat potential customers into buying from him and scare tactics and vulgar language to terrorize his colleagues into better performance. The core tenet of his philosophy is to always be closing. According to Blake, it doesn't matter who the prospect is, where the lead comes from, what their needs are, or whether your product or service is right for them. The only thing that matters is doing his job, which is to bring in the money and close the deal, no matter what.

This kind of garbage might have worked in the '80s or '90s, but fast-forward to today, and things are a lot different from what they used to be, thankfully. The sad part is that you still see these soulless, ABC fake gurus we discussed earlier who continue to peddle their magic selling systems, fool-proof funnels, and Ponzi scheme–like real estate funds to put you on the path to riches by next week.

If you're a sales professional who wants to build a reputation based on integrity, honor, conscientiousness, and caring, you can use a couple of strategies that embody the *always-be-helping* mantra. First, determine whether your prospect has a problem you can solve. If they have no reason to buy what you have or no ability to use your particular product or service, why would you waste your time (and theirs) talking to them?

You should *never* sell something to someone who doesn't need what you're offering. If you or your prospect come to the conclusion it's not going to work out, you can save each other time, energy, and money by letting them know you can't help everybody and it's just not a good fit. Too many salespeople spend time on unqualified leads and prospects without realizing how much time they're wasting—time they could spend on quality leads and qualified prospects. If you focus on the right prospects by finding your ideal clients, you'll improve your effectiveness tremendously.

Closing without "Closing"

You need to understand something very important before you can close effectively. (I'm only using the word "closing," which I hate, because it's been ingrained in our heads for decades.) Let's change the word "closing" to the phrase "offer to help." A very important part of the offer to help is called the "why change" message. I learned this from one of the best salespeople I've ever met, David Weiss. Delivering the "why change" message is almost like a State of the Union address for the situation. We need to establish the prospect's current state, meaning where they are right now in their business. We then need to dive into what their future state would look like in an ideal world. Next, we need to eloquently reveal the gap between their current and future states. And last, we need to make the value of bridging that gap abundantly clear.

Why should you have this consultative, caring, and *always-be-helping* mentality in sales? Because the balance of power has been tipped away from salespeople and now favors the prospects. An enormous amount of information is available online today, which means that prospects are more informed and savvier than they used to be. The high-pressure sales tactics and one-call close methods don't work anymore because most people know they don't need to buy right now. They know that they have several different options, several different solutions, and several different vendors that can provide something similar to what you provide.

You would think that sales training companies would understand this and try to teach things that help salespeople separate themselves from the rank-and-file old-school sellers. Nope, they don't. The most famous peddler of magic selling systems still teaches tactics from sixty years ago, which are some of the worst selling techniques I've ever seen. Even worse than that, salespeople are taught to ask idiotic, imbecilic, and manipulative closing questions, which should somehow magically make prospects buy from you. Give me a f**king break.

They're taught to say things like, "What can I do to put you in this car today, Carmen?" Or "Is there anything that would stop us from moving forward today, Indra?" Stop. That's garbage. Many salespeople really do say things like this, and they actually think it works. (Sigh.)

So, what should you say? How do you sell more effectively? Remember what you learned in chapter one. Before you can confidently convert a prospect into a buyer, you need to ask *yourself* the following questions: Do I understand my prospect? Do I understand their business? Their market? Their goals for the business? Their schedule for fixing this issue? How would staying the same impact their bottom line or their life? Am I confident I can help them? Are we the right fit for them? Are there any red flags? These are all questions you should ask yourself and have the answers to before you confidently attempt to ask for their business.

Your prospects will also have questions, and they'll need answers before they'll be ready to make a decision and be closable. They'll have questions like these: Do I trust them? Do I like them? Do they understand my exact situation? Can they really help us? Are they an expert in their field? Is their company reputable? Are they worth what they charge? Can they make my life easier? Your goal is to provide those answers in your presentation and build massive value.

You must understand that the first half of the entire closing process starts with you asking questions about them to see whether they're even available for closing. The second half includes them asking questions about you to see whether they're even a potential user of your product or service. After you've done that, it's time to ask for their business, which, again, is not done by asking a foolish closing question. This is so simple, but most salespeople complicate things and try to figure out what specific closing questions or techniques will work best. Don't waste your time on that. It's not necessary, and it doesn't work.

Remember the question I shared with you in chapter one.

"So, where do we go from here?"

Straightforward, to the point, and either they'll say, "Let's do it," or they'll give you a reason why they're not sold yet. Based on their answer, we know where to go from there. You can try to handle their objections, if they have any, at this point. But of course, we're hoping they'll just say yes and give you the green light to move forward and get the deal done. Remember, closing is not about manipulation, pressure, or old-school tactics. Learn how to build massive amounts of value into your presentation, and you'll be surprised by how many more deals you close without having to close.

True sales professionals treat their prospects and clients with care, respect, and appreciation. True sales professionals aren't out to get whatever they can. They're not drooling over monthly bonuses, boats, or twenty-thousand-dollar watches. Let's do our best to ignore all this ABC junk, continue to learn and become students of consumer behavior, and treat prospects like fellow human beings. If we do that, maybe someday, people will look at a career in sales as something to be proud of. I certainly am.

SALESPEOPLE AND MUSHROOMS

THIS CHAPTER IS INTENDED FOR SALES MANAGERS, but I'm sure the salespeople out there will be shaking their heads as they read it, just like I'm shaking my head as I write it. Here's a question for you. What do salespeople and mushrooms have in common? Although you may already have the answer, take a second to think about it. I've asked tens of thousands of people this question, and I can't tell you how many different answers I've received. Here are some of the most common answers:

- They're fun guys. (Rimshot noise.)
- They hallucinate a lot.
- They make me want to do drugs.
- They're big-headed.
- They're dirty.

I could keep going, but some of the answers are R-rated and should never be put into print. There is one common answer I hear the most, though: They're fed s**t and kept in the dark.

Unfortunately, most of the salespeople reading this book have already heard this and can clearly relate to that statement. But why? Why is this so commonplace, and why do most of us know exactly what that means? It's because that's the way it's always been. Teach salespeople enough to be dangerous and to keep the money coming in—that's all they're good for, and that's all they need to know. It's quite ironic when you consider that salespeople are yelled at, demeaned, humiliated, and publicly shamed for giving away margin or profit. Yet they're never told what the margin or profit actually is, so they have no idea how much they're giving away.

One of the best business practices I've come across in my forty-seven years of life is transparency. Transparency eliminates the whole mushroom thing with salespeople. Imagine what would happen if a company knowingly and intentionally educated its entire staff about how the business works. What would happen if company leaders taught their employees about the supply chain, cost of goods sold, profit margin, expenses, and EBITDA? Can you fathom a situation where salespeople know how their bonuses are calculated, how they can all work as a team to achieve them, and how valuable it is for all staff members to be fully aligned at all times? Crazy, huh?

I don't have time to get into the endless number of benefits that transparent leadership can provide to your organization, but we will talk about how it relates to salespeople. If I'm in sales, I'm most likely paid based on the revenue I generate. I know that's not true in all compensation plans, but it's true for most salespeople. Some companies do understand that margin or gross profit is more important than revenue, so they have tailored their compensation plans to those parameters rather than gross revenue. But if you're not one of those companies and you do pay your salespeople on total revenue generated, you can't be upset when they give away margin, make you less profit, or discount their deals. In a later chapter, we discuss why this is also tied to hindrances in their Sales DNA (based on our assessment called The Sales DNA Test).

We live in a society of blame, and that's unfortunate. Parents blame teachers when their kids get low grades. Fans blame referees when their team loses a big game. Networks blame time slots when their shows don't receive high ratings. Our society has an endless stream of people who blame everybody else for their misfortunes in life. It is mind-boggling how many people on this planet blame every single person for their lack of results—except the person in the mirror, who's really the only one responsible. The blame game is destroying companies from within, and it can permeate the entire organization. Whether you're a sales leader or a salesperson, you get blamed. Sales managers get blamed for their sales team's poor performance. Salespeople blame the sales managers for their poor performance. Each of them blames leadership for failing to do their jobs effectively. If it's everyone else's fault all the time, how will anything ever be improved?

Let's start with the excuse-laden salespeople. These are the complainers, excuse-makers, and woe-is-me people. In a coaching session with a client's sales team, I asked each of them why sales were down and why they weren't as effective as they could be. The first salesperson said he wasn't as frustrated as much as he was disappointed. I asked him why.

He said, "Customers just aren't buying."

I was saddened but not surprised. Apparently, it was the customer's fault that he wasn't selling. I asked him if he really and truly believed that was the reason.

He shouted at me, "It's the truth!"

I said to him, "It's *your* truth, not *the* truth."

When you start blaming your customers for not buying from you and take zero responsibility for not providing massive amounts of value and a great presentation, guess what? Your chances of being successful in the sales profession are quite small. Unfortunately, in sales, especially over the past decade, you could skate by, survive, fly under the radar, and still make a hundred grand.

Exacerbating this issue is the lack of accountability in many sales organizations. There's even less training and coaching than there used to be, and all too often, substandard performers are allowed to meander along while remaining employed year after year. Aggravating this issue is the almost nonexistent onboarding for new salespeople, who are expected to perform at world-class levels of competence with no guidance, no sales process to follow, and no system of checks and balances to ensure they ramp up quickly.

How does this lead to complacency? As the incomparable Ron Livingston, who plays Peter Gibbons from Initech in the movie *Office Space*, eloquently put it, ". . . my only real motivation is not to be hassled, that, and the fear of losing my job. But you know, Bob, that'll only make someone work just hard enough not to get fired."[1]

This can be extremely frustrating for sales managers, and that's understandable. Many of them ask the same questions of their salespeople. Where's the *drive*? Where's the *effort*, the *passion*, the *work ethic*, the *everything you've got*?! You can't just wing it in sales, go through the motions, and expect to be a top performer. You can't be a lazy deflector who blames the world for your problems and then thinks you're going to excel. The crazy part is that salespeople seem to have endless hours to binge-stream, scroll through TikTok, and play video games, but they can't find the time to read, learn, study, skill-build, or master the craft of professional selling. Still, they always seem to find someone to blame for their poor results. If you're not getting the results you want, guess what?

You May Be the Problem. You, and You Alone.

If you're not happy where you are in life at this very moment, maybe it's time to take a long look at yourself in the mirror and commit to investing the work it's going to take to get you where you want to be. *Stop making excuses* and blaming everybody else for why you're not there.

Let's switch gears and dive into the reasons why sales managers underperform. Of course, there's no way it could ever be their fault, so guess who they blame when the numbers are down. Their salespeople! I know, I know, I just talked about the mediocre, lazy, order-taking blamers who permeate sales organizations around the world. But even with a team fraught with excuse-makers, it often falls back on the sales leader when the sales team is unsuccessful.

Let me give you an example outside the sales world to illustrate this point. Let's say you're going to teach your four-year-old daughter how to ride a bike. Most parents would probably begin by buying her a small bike with training wheels to help her get the hang of the balance. They'd find an open space with lots of room to ride without a car in sight. They'd make sure their daughter wore her knee pads, elbow pads, and helmet. (Some of you are laughing because if you grew up like me and with a father like mine, there was none of that!) The next steps are helping her get on the bike, holding on tight, and telling her, "Daddy's right here, okay?" And they hold the back of her seat and handlebars and tell her to keep pedaling, no matter what. You're getting the visual now, and it may be bringing back some nice memories. ☺ That's more or less how many parents taught their children how to ride a bike.

But in sales, here's pretty much how it goes: "The bike is in the garage. Make sure you wear your helmet. Daddy will be here watching a movie, but I believe in you. You got this! Yell if you need anything, okay?" I really do wish I was kidding, but I'm not.

One of the leading causes of failure for new salespeople is the lack of effective onboarding they receive. It takes the average salesperson ten months to ramp up, which means companies must invest significant resources (both time and money) to ensure each salesperson becomes a profitable entity for their organization. Did you know the median length of onboarding time for a new salesperson in the United States is three days?! Less than one week is all salespeople get before they're expected to perform at a high level and hit the unrealistic quota they've been assigned.

Huh? What? Yes, those are the facts. Do you know how long it takes to become a barber in the United States? Take a guess. Depending on the state, it takes between eight hundred and one thousand hours. In addition to spending half a year learning this skill, you've got to invest roughly $5K to $15K, complete all the necessary training and coursework, and then pass an exam! All to become a barber. How about becoming a lawyer? How long does that take? Well, typically, four years of undergrad and another three years of law school. You will also need to invest roughly $300K and then pass the bar examination.

How about a physician? How long does that take? Physicians have between five and ten years of onboarding before they're allowed to practice medicine. But the average salesperson gets less than one week and is expected to become proficient and deliver amazing results?!

Effective onboarding reduces ramp-up time, reduces turnover and recruiting costs, improves employee retention, enhances company culture, and ensures your customers have a positive experience. By providing your new salespeople with proper onboarding comprising the right training, guidance, tools, resources, and support, you'll create a strong foundation for long-term success and growth.

They'll Be Just Fine

We all know what happens when you assume: It makes an a** out of you and me. And unfortunately, this happens way too much in companies when it comes to new salespeople and why they aren't onboarded properly. Here are just a few of the assumptions made by company leaders:

- They know what they're doing.
- They've been in sales for twenty years.
- They don't need us micromanaging them.
- They'll fit seamlessly into our culture.
- They'll eventually learn about our product/service.
- They were successful in their last company.
- They're a quick learner; they'll get it.
- They don't need us watching over them.

- They're naturally talented; we can leave them alone.

- They're a senior-level salesperson.

- They have industry experience.

- They don't need onboarding.

- They don't need coaching.

- They don't need training.

- They don't need to be held accountable.

- They don't need feedback.

- They don't need encouragement.

- They don't need to work on personal development.

- They don't need to meet the other staff here.

This attitude defies logic, yet it's applied every day to thousands of newly hired salespeople. Leaders make assumptions about salespeople based on old-school thinking, and they can't figure out why their teams are underperforming. If your strategy for growth is to leave your salespeople alone and assume they'll be fine, here's what you're in for.

High Turnover

According to HubSpot, the average turnover rate (churn) among salespeople is 35 percent. The average turnover rate among non-sales-related employees is 12 percent. Put another way, around one-third of your salespeople will leave your organization in the upcoming year. Considering that the ideal churn rate for an organization's employees is around 10 percent, turnover for salespeople reaches far beyond the average.[2] Salespeople who receive little to no support, training, or coaching are more likely to become frustrated, disengaged, unproductive, and jaded, and they will quickly leave their organizations.

Poor and Inconsistent Performance

Without proper onboarding, training, coaching, support, and feedback, many salespeople will struggle to meet their targets, fulfill the company's expectations, and achieve their full potential in sales. More importantly, if you allow salespeople to figure it all out on their own, they'll develop their own approaches to selling, which will lead to inconsistent messaging, incongruent processes, and poor customer experiences.

Customer Dissatisfaction and Brand Damage

These two go hand in hand: When your customers have a bad experience, they tell ten times more people about it than they do about a great experience. Salespeople who are not adequately trained and coached will cause immense damage. If they don't know all the ins and outs of what you do, they will provide inaccurate information to customers, they'll make stuff up, they'll embellish, they'll lie, and they'll make promises they cannot deliver. I think you understand why this will infuriate your customers and cause irreparable brand damage, from which you may never recover.

Inefficient Sales Processes

The Sales Management Association, a "global, cross-industry professional association for managers in sales force effectiveness," conducted extensive research on the importance of a guided sales process. According to their findings, "90% of all companies that use a formal, guided sales process were ranked as the highest performing."[3] If you are not training your salespeople to execute the steps of a sales process in chronological order, every time, you'll pay a serious price. Not following a sales process will cause much longer sales cycles, higher costs of sale, fewer deals, lower margins, lower win rates, inaccurate forecasts, and inconsistent results.

Destruction of Your Culture

Intentional or not, neglecting the needed development and support of your salespeople will create an extremely negative culture within your sales team. If you have a team composed of individuals who feel alone, isolated, and unsupported, your organization is in for a world of hurt. Toxic sales cultures take a long time to fix, and if poor leadership is the main cause, it may never change. If morale is low, salespeople will be disengaged, their trust will be fleeting, they won't give 100 percent, they'll walk at the bell, and turnover will be alarmingly high.

I could go on and on about the mistreatment of salespeople and how that leads to low performance, but this should be enough for you to understand that treating your salespeople like mushrooms is not a good idea. If salespeople are left to fend for themselves without adequate support, training, coaching, and guidance, it will cause devastation in your organization if it hasn't already. Sales managers, please take this message to heart and invest in ongoing training, coaching, tools, systems, and technology to better support your salespeople and foster a culture of continuous improvement, collaboration, and growth.

Creating a Team of Sunflowers

Instead of treating your salespeople like mushrooms, how about treating them like sunflowers? Why sunflowers? Well, for starters, everyone loves sunflowers! They make you smile; they're big, bold, and beautiful and add color and vibrance to their surroundings. This is exactly how most salespeople would be described, right? (Eye roll.) You can probably figure out how sunflowers got their name. Their scientific genus is *Helianthus*. This comes from the Greek words for sun (*helios*) and flower (*anthus*). Young sunflowers face the sun as it moves through the sky to soak up all that sunshine to grow.

Listen up, sales managers: If you truly want your salespeople to grow tall, strong, and vibrant, you've got to look to the sunflower for inspiration. If you want to build a powerful sales team, look to the sunflower (as Jerry Seinfeld taught us to "look to the cookie, Elaine, look to the cookie!"). Here are five ways to treat your salespeople like sunflowers.

Be Their Sunlight

In order for sunflowers to grow, they need ample amounts of sunlight every day. Six to eight hours each day provide all the energy and life-giving forces they need to survive and thrive. Much like sunflowers need sun, salespeople need sales managers. Sales managers can be the difference between a bright, growing, and vibrant salesperson or a wilting, moping, and dying salesperson. You must always think about how you can be the ray of light in their lives and provide all the tools and encouragement they need to grow. Ultimately, it's up to you whether they live or die.

Plant Properly for More Fruitful Harvests

Just as you would carefully select the ideal spot to plant sunflower seeds, it's crucial to choose the right candidates for your sales team. You need to plant them in the right soil, at the right time of year, and in the right spot if you want to have a successful harvest. It's the same for salespeople. You need to provide a supportive environment, take care of their individual needs, and put them in the right role to ensure they have the chance to reach their full potential.

Start with Good Soil

You can't plant sunflower seeds in sand and expect them to grow. You must plant them in the right soil to give them a fighting chance. Most salespeople are treated like sunflower seeds spit out by baseball players in the dugout. Wherever they land, they land. Someone eventually comes along and sweeps them up after the game, half-eaten, discarded, and stepped on. Only a select few luckily flutter in the air long enough to bounce off the top step of the dugout and land safely in the grass. As a sales leader, you must provide the soil your salespeople need to thrive in from the second they start with you. Proper onboarding (not three days like the average company), proper support, proper encouragement, proper training, proper expectations, and proper coaching should be nonnegotiable in your company when it comes to new salespeople.

Water Them!

Sunflowers need a consistent and plentiful supply of water. Sunflowers like daily routines, especially when it comes to water. They need to be watered regularly in the early stages of life to encourage rapid growth. Do that with your salespeople. Much like sunflowers in the early stages of their lives, salespeople, early on in their employment with you, need daily routines consisting of training, coaching, support, and feedback. These *must be ongoing processes*! You can't water a sunflower once a quarter and expect it to grow. Unfortunately, tons of sales managers think like this and believe that a once-a-quarter soaking with a fifty-five-gallon drum of water will somehow make their salespeople grow.

Feed Them, and They'll Feed You

Not only are sunflowers aesthetically beautiful, they also provide food for hundreds of millions of people. Sunflower seeds are full of nutrients, proteins, and vitamins, as well as healthy fats and carbs. Sunflowers are used in oils, salads, teas, and many other ways. By nurturing and caring for your salespeople, you will create an environment for them to grow, bloom, thrive, and produce. By helping them reach and achieve their full potential, you'll be the farmer responsible for incredible harvest after incredible harvest that feeds your organization with revenue, repeat clients, and profitability for decades to come. Salespeople who work in supportive and nurturing environments are more energetic, enthusiastic, coachable, engaged, aligned, and productive.

You can treat your salespeople like mushrooms—keep them in the dark and feed them s**t—or you can treat them like sunflowers and invest in their growth and development to ensure they produce results. If you do the latter, you will have a team of confident, competent, and hardworking salespeople who can handle any situation that arises. You'll have a sales team excited to come to work every day because it's abundantly clear their company is investing in their future growth and success. You'll have a team of salespeople who look forward to role-play and are pumped to attend their sales meetings rather than dreading them. You'll be better able to hold your team accountable because they'll feel the need to return the favor of the time and energy you invested into meeting their needs. And finally, you'll now have a culture of coaching, personal growth, and mentorship, which ultimately drives higher performance and better results.

PROSPECTING PROFICIENCY LEADS TO PROLIFIC PROFITS

I FOUND A LIVING, BREATHING HUMAN! That must mean they're a prospect, right? Wrong. I can't tell you how many times salespeople sell their products or services to the wrong prospects, wrong targets, and wrong customers. I sincerely wish I had learned what I'm about to share with you twenty-five years ago.

Just Because You Can, It Doesn't Mean You Should

Here's what I wish I had learned a while back: Just because somebody wants to buy something from you doesn't mean you should sell it to them.

This flies in the face of everything holy in sales, doesn't it? Well, when you have organizations that still don't seem to understand that not all revenue is *good* revenue, this continues to happen. When an organization's sole goal is to sell as much as possible and drive revenue at all costs, this isn't surprising. Here are just a few of the things that happen when you sell to the *wrong* prospects.

Lower Conversion Rates

Wait. Don't companies want their salespeople to sell more stuff? Yes. Does selling to the wrong prospects lead to fewer sales? Yes! If you're selling to people who aren't your ideal customers, they'll have fewer problems for you to fix, they'll lack the understanding of why you do what you do, and they'll see less value in your product or service. All of these factors clearly lead to fewer sales.

Here's one example: If you're selling software to middle-market manufacturing companies and your target prospect is the CEO, and eight of your last ten demos have been with startup companies in the fintech space, you will see lower conversion rates. Why? It's the wrong industry, wrong company size, and wrong decision-maker. This happens all the time, and it's the sales manager's job to dive deeper into the numbers, not just berate their salespeople because their conversion rates are low.

Wasted Time and Resources

When you spend time on the wrong prospects, it's twice as damaging as you think. Not only are you wasting time with folks who probably won't buy from you, but you're also losing that time for people who *will* buy from you. Your team (marketing, fulfillment, procurement, warehouse) will also lose the time they spent helping you acquire and support customers you should never have sold to in the first place.

Let's expand on the previous example. If you're selling software to middle-market manufacturing companies and you waste time on prospects outside your Ideal Customer Profile (ICP), you'll not only have lower conversion rates, but you'll also have fewer opportunities to be referred to middle-market manufacturing companies. If you do a great job and provide excellent service along with tremendous value, your clients will gladly make introductions for you without you having to ask. Do you want introductions to other ideal prospects who are already warm and in your target market, or do you want introductions to the wrong people in the wrong companies in the wrong industries?

Brand Damage

We cover this in Chapter 4, and I can't say it enough: If you sell to the wrong people, your brand will be damaged more than you think. You could do everything perfectly. You could deliver on time, exceed expectations, and give them the deal of a lifetime. But if it's the wrong type of customer or client, they'll find something wrong. They won't care about the ninety-nine things you did right. They'll complain (publicly on social media) about what a horrible company you work for and claim that you're the worst salesperson on Earth.

Why would you provide exemplary customer service and world-class value to someone who didn't really need or want your service or product in the first place? Why would you waste your time on that? To make money? To hit some arbitrary quota? If you sell the right thing to the wrong people or the wrong thing to the right people, not much good can come of it. For example, you could cook a five-star duck à l'orange that would win awards, but if you accidentally served it to a vegetarian who's the CEO of PETA, you may not get the positive feedback and review you're accustomed to. That word will spread, especially if they take to social media, and that one sale may cost you millions.

Diminished Morale

As leaders, you want your salespeople to be positive, motivated, happy, and feel like they are part of a winning culture. It's pretty difficult to do that when salespeople are demotivated, disappointed, desperate, and continually rejected. And what do you think happens when you sell to the wrong prospects? Exactly that. Selling to the wrong prospects will cause more rejection, more frustration, more anxiety, and more disappointment.

I recently shared this in a workshop with a group of CEOs, and one of them blurted out, "Steve, I don't want happy salespeople. I want results."

I paused because I was about to tell him what I really thought, but I decided not to. Instead, I stood in silence, let what he said sink in for the rest of the CEOs in the room, and then one of them said, "Mike, did you really just say that?"

I won't go into what the rest of that discussion was like, but let's just say some people are completely out of touch with reality and the world we're living in.

If you like to fish, like I do, but you don't know where to go, what lures to use, what gear to bring, or how to cast, you may get frustrated. If you cast and cast and cast, hour after hour, and you don't get so much as a nibble, you'll start to lose confidence. You'll start the negative self-talk, you'll get more frustrated as the minutes pass, you'll be less inclined to enjoy the experience, and you might even snap the fishing rod in half over your knee. This experience doesn't exactly incite positive feelings about fishing, which reduces the chances that you'll ever enjoy or become good at and excited about fishing again.

This is just a small sampling of the damage caused by selling to the wrong prospects. The importance of selling to the *right prospects* cannot be understated, and if you want to avoid all these negative consequences, you've got to define and sell to your ideal customers. They will be the ones who align with your message and branding, who really need what you offer and know you can help them, and who will welcome your product or service into their lives and businesses. This is known as your ICP, and selling to these folks is crucial to the future success of your organization.

Defining Your Ideal Customer Profile (ICP)

Now that we know to whom we should *not* be selling, let's talk about the value of defining your ICP. In any aspect of life, you've got to identify what you're looking for if you want to find it. Defining your ideal customer is critical to your success in sales. Sales is not about throwing a bunch of stuff against the wall and seeing what sticks. Sales is *not* simply a numbers game. Sales is a skills game. It's about having a targeted prospecting practice and knowing who you're trying to reach exactly.

Why is that so important? Because it will save you time in the long run. You can't just have the hit-and-hope mentality, contact a thousand random people, book some random meetings, and pray a few of them give you some money. You've got to focus your prospecting efforts and target your ideal clients. Your ideal clients are the ones who are more likely to buy from you. They'll buy from you in less time and without price complaints, they'll have fewer objections and be more responsive, and they'll refer other people to you who are just like them!

It's critical to operate this way to build a lasting brand, become more profitable, increase enterprise value, and continue operating the business successfully for decades to come. The following are six steps that will help you identify your ideal customer.

Step One: Who Is Your Ideal Customer, and What Do They Look Like?

To define your ideal customer, you must first determine their demographics and psychographics. Demographics can be used as a starting point to find that ideal customer, and they're defined as common themes and characteristics based on particular groups of people. Psychographics are the second identifying factor you can use, and they determine the where, the why, and the what. In B2B sales, demographics may include industry type, location, company revenue, employee size, years in business, and even corporate culture. In B2C sales, demographics may include gender, neighborhood, annual income, marital status, and employment status. Psychographics are generally the same for B2B and B2C: What are your ideal prospects' personalities? What are their values, attitudes, interests, and lifestyles? Using the common denominators of demographics and psychographics helps you identify your ideal clients and customers and puts you on a better path to success.

For example, if you're selling solar in the B2C space, you need to focus on the people who fit your ICP so they're more likely to recognize your value and buy from you. It could be homeowners on the South Shore of Massachusetts with a household income of $150K to $200K who own electric vehicles, are college-educated, and have lived in the home for more than five years. If you're selling fractional CFO services in the B2B space, your focus may be on companies with $10M to $50M in annual revenue in the metro Detroit automotive manufacturing space who need to raise capital, improve profitability, and improve financial health.

You can use a variety of tools, both free and paid, to gather this data and information. This can include company websites, social media, research firms, public information, surveys, census data, administrative records, and much more.

Step Two: What Are Their Problems and Challenges?

No matter what you sell, whether it's medical devices, insurance, memberships, or SaaS, you're selling the solution to a problem. Plain and simple. People want to know *how* you're going to solve their problems. People want to achieve, acquire, and avoid certain things, and they're looking for results that your product, service, or solution will need to provide. You've got to conduct deep discovery (which we'll cover shortly) to help them identify their problems and challenges so you can clearly illustrate your ability to solve them.

The top five percenters in sales take this a step further. They're so good at discovery they often uncover problems their prospects never knew they had. Asking deep, probing, and challenging questions is one way to accomplish this. Another way is to master the AQ technique (Answer Intelligence), which teaches you specific ways to *answer* questions and not just how to ask them. This is the key to becoming a world-class sales professional. If you're a sales leader, I'm imploring you to spend the time it takes to develop a discovery process that will set your team apart from every other sales team out there.

The easiest and cheapest way to find out the common problems and challenges of your target audience is to ask your existing customers. What problems were they facing? What challenges did they have difficulty overcoming? You can also research industry publications through Google searches and industry associations on LinkedIn and many other sources. If you can compile enough data on this topic, you'll know what your target's competitors and colleagues are dealing with, and you can tailor your message and value proposition to address those specific issues.

Step Three: What Specific Benefits and Solutions Are They Looking For?

Of all the benefits you offer, which are the most important to your ideal customer? What are the most pressing needs that your product or service satisfies? Why should your customer buy from you rather than from someone else? How will your product or service make their life easier? How much time have you spent asking your customers these questions? Do you really know, or are you just assuming? Similar to the advice I gave in the last section, you must take the time to research and speak with your customers. Why did they originally seek you out? Why did they hire you, specifically? What are the benefits they've received so far that have helped them the most? Find out exactly what your ideal prospects are looking for, then devise and develop a strategy to provide it to them!

Step Four: How Do They Want to Be Approached?

First, you must understand the demands and expectations of your ideal customers. Then, you must discover ways to address those demands and expectations during their interactions with your business. Do they always buy right away, or do they buy after a trial offer? Do they buy at the beginning or end of their fiscal year? Do they need the approval of the C-suite, procurement, or HR? Do they prefer email communication, phone conversations, or face-to-face interaction? Do they respond to more or fewer interactions with you or your company? Do they want incentives, lower prices, or better service? Do they buy more frequently through a time-based offer, or do they buy more within a relaxed and slower sales cycle? Understanding all these factors is critical to identifying your ideal customer. If you don't know the answers to these questions, what exactly are you relying on to increase results?

Talk to your customers. Ask them what they liked about your outreach, follow-up, and pursuit of their business. You can also ask them what they don't like about the approaches they receive from vampire-like salespeople who incessantly beg them for their business. If you can compile enough data from your ideal customers and know what they hate, you know what not to do! If you can find out how they prefer to be approached, you know what you need to do!

Step Five: What Value Do They See in Your Product/ Service/Solution?

It's imperative that you find out exactly what your customers value most. Ask them because this helps you discover your true differentiator. Is it the high quality of your product or service? Is it because your staff members are super friendly and attentive? Is it that they achieve faster results with your help? Is it your responsiveness or your availability? Is it your speedy delivery or fulfillment? Find out what your true value is to your customers, and once you discover what that is, design a plan to deliver that value in even better ways. You've got to spend the time necessary to understand exactly how your ideal customers think. Then, and only then, will you be able to determine what their values are. If you want to reach your full potential in sales, you've got to illustrate and demonstrate why you're different in the way your ideal customers want and value. More often than not, your customers will value and appreciate all the little things you do to show why you're different from your competition.

As we wrap up this section, put yourself in the shoes of a top one percenter in sales (you may already be there). Here's what they know before they ever approach a prospect:

- They know the exact demographics and psychographics of their ideal prospect.

- Out of ten thousand potential prospects, they know which five hundred prospects are ideal, and that's who they focus on.

- They know that higher conversion rates, higher average deal size, shorter sales cycles, and longer engagement terms are waiting for them when selling to these ideal prospects.

- They know the most common problems and challenges these prospects deal with, and they construct their entire sales process from beginning to end with this in mind.

- They know how these prospects prefer to be approached and exactly how *not* to approach them. This gives them the upper hand in the competition with those who spray and pray, hoping to set appointments.

- They already know the budgets and financial allocations for investments in similar services, so they can adequately and eloquently provide value throughout the sales process and appropriately position their solution.

Step Six: How Do You Identify and Target Decision-Makers?

Identifying and targeting your ideal decision-maker isn't always a straightforward process because it's not always obvious who this person is. It may be more than one person, and it may take substantial time and effort to determine the right person. As we all know, the decision-maker has the power to make or break the deal. Think of it this way: The decision-maker is the person who can wire the money, make the deal move faster, and get the right parties involved, or they can put the kibosh on your deal.

One of the ways you can gather this information is by asking questions during the discovery phase. Who could put a stop to this deal immediately? Who could speed this thing up? Who could mitigate the number of boards, committees, or panels you need to meet? In the past, when they purchased a solution like yours, who gave the final stamp of approval?

Questions like these can save you a ton of time and help you refine your message to get you in front of the final decision-maker faster. If the person you're speaking with isn't the final decision-maker, you can find out who really holds the power in this potential deal through this line of questioning. These are just a few ways to find out from your first contact, your internal champion, or a stakeholder who the real decision-maker is and then better understand how to navigate toward that person.

What happens if you can't identify or get in front of the decision-maker? What do you do now? Failing to reach the decision-maker will clearly slow or stall the sales process, and it will cause you to miss out on providing solutions you know can help your client. It can also increase the chances that your competition can outmaneuver you, and of course, it can cost you an untold number of deals, revenue, and income. You must have a strategic approach to reaching the ultimate decision-maker to maximize your chances of success in sales.

Locating the decision-maker is not always an easy process. However, by doing your research, befriending the gatekeeper, asking the right questions, looking for clues, using LinkedIn and other sites, and leveraging your champions, you can substantially increase your chances of connecting with the ultimate decision-maker and closing that deal.

The first and simplest way to start is by visiting their company website. Often, the decision-maker is on the senior leadership team and will most likely be featured on the website.

The second way you can identify the decision-maker is to ask the gatekeeper or a point of contact for help. Something like, "Hey, I'm trying to reach Art Vandelay, and I know he's extremely busy. I have in my notes here that Art makes the decisions regarding x, y, and z. Is that right, or am I off base here?" *Befriending* the gatekeeper is essential, and—pay attention here—it's not about *getting past* the gatekeeper. The gatekeeper can confirm whether you're on track and provide you with valuable information that may lead you to the ultimate decision-maker.

In my Aflac days, I would take a sincere interest in the gatekeepers, find out who they were and what was going on in their life that day, and act like a normal human being. When I stopped by in person, I'd bring them something I knew they liked based on a previous conversation. Maybe it was a candy bar, maybe it was a book, and in some cases, it was a stuffed Aflac duck. ☺ Once they knew I was a fellow human being who wasn't just trying to *get past* them, they would tell me not only who the decision-maker was, but they'd often walk me right in or insist on setting up the meeting for me.

Third, you can use a tool like LinkedIn Sales Navigator (or one of several other tools), which usually has full organization charts mapped out, including a company's leadership structure. If you know your ICP well enough and understand your ideal targets, you can make educated guesses about who the decision-maker might be. You can also look at their LinkedIn profile, research the company page, search through the pages of other employees who have profiles on LinkedIn, or even look through the LinkedIn groups they're part of to see whether you can find any inside information.

Finally, you can always think outside the box. We worked with a company in the agricultural space that sold water meters to farmers. One of their salespeople wanted to find the owner of one particular farm, so he started looking on social media. He ended up finding out who it was from his normal Facebook page, and he noticed the guy was a huge San Francisco Giants fan. A few weeks later, he went to the farm and saw a guy in a San Francisco Giants hat loading a truck. He knew that was Ted, the owner, so he slowly approached and said softly,

"Excuse me, sir, are you Ted?" That research sparked a conversation that led to a $500K order.

Making Better Connections with the Decision-Makers

Now that you know the value of identifying the right decision-makers, I'd like to share six strategies you can implement to help you connect with them better.

Six Strategies to Better Connect with Decision-Makers

- Leverage your network.
- Use multiple channels.
- Be professionally persistent.
- Provide value.
- Build relationships.
- Become an expert.

Let's begin with the first strategy, leveraging your network. Don't just think about this as your online or social media network. Of course, LinkedIn plays a huge role in your business networking ability, and that's essential if you're in the B2B space. You'll want to leverage your mutual connections, find out who they're connected to (your second-degree connections), and see whether there's someone you know who can connect you to them. You can also reach out to connections you may already have inside the company. You can ask your colleagues if they know anyone at your particular target companies. And don't forget to use your network of friends. Many times, we fail to realize that our personal connections have business connections that we'd like to meet. Obviously, a warmer connection to a decision-maker is best, so here's a quick example of how to ask for a warm introduction from someone you know:

"Hey Juan, I was looking at our mutual connections and I saw that you're connected to [Name], and I'd love an intro. Would you mind connecting us, if possible?"

That's it. Simple. If they trust you with their network and you've already proven that you can deliver value, they'll be more open to making that connection for you.

Number two, use multiple channels. A pitcher in baseball doesn't throw one pitch every time, and a football team doesn't run one play every time. But all too often, salespeople rely on just one communication channel to attempt to reach a decision-maker: always calling, always emailing, always messaging via LinkedIn, etc. You've got to mix it up! You've got to reach out a lot, and you've got to use different combinations of cadences. You may even want to send them lumpy mail (mailing physical items) or write them a quick letter (yes, *write* with a pen in your hand). You could stop by in person and bring cookies or lunch. That's less common these days, but it's still done in quite a few industries.

The third strategy for connecting with decision-makers more successfully is to be professionally persistent. If you're in sales, you must realize it's not easy to get in touch with decision-makers, and you most certainly can't rely on one lucky call or email and think that's a good long-term plan. Decision-makers purposely try to avoid salespeople at all costs, and some even have lines of defense set up to do just that. They have spam filters set up in their email, they employ gatekeepers, and they temper their LinkedIn check-ins so most people won't see your first message. It takes time, effort, multiple channels, and persistence to master this crucial aspect of selling.

What does professionally persistent mean? It means you need to be persistent enough that people eventually feel compelled to respond to you and believe me, they'll respect your stick-to-itiveness. But there's a fine line between persistent and annoying. Remember, if their first thought is to call the police and not you, you've gone too far. Don't stalk people! Decision-makers are busy people, so it's essential to be pleasantly persistent but respectful. You've got to follow up a lot but don't be overly pushy or too aggressive.

Number four is to provide value. When you connect with a decision-maker, have something to say! Have a plan—something you've crafted and practiced—based on your ICP. You must provide something of value, or they'll have no reason to meet with you. Show them you understand their challenges and that you may have some solutions that can help them. This is an example of something you can say to show your value.

"Typically, when I'm working with other CROs/HR directors/ individuals like yourself, they're facing these kinds of problems (share one or two common problems for their role, industry, etc.). What we've discovered is if they do X, Y, and Z, it really impacts their (whatever you want to say here, based on their business). I'm curious to get your thoughts on that."

As a reminder, these aren't magic scripts! You may like them, and you may not. You may want to use them or change them up. It's okay! But you've got to add some insight or knowledge. You've got to demonstrate some expertise or competency. You need to show them you provide value and that you're not the typical salesperson spewing regurgitated, appointment-setting lines or asking them to buy something. You can also share some insider information, demonstrate that you know their industry and what problems they're facing, and ask for their thoughts or input. Most people like to give their opinion on just about anything—just ask them. You can also send them any articles, videos, or podcasts that feature you to show them your expertise or industry insights. The most important part is this: don't pitch them! They've already been pitched enough, probably that same day. Sometimes, it's best to offer content, information, or help without asking for an appointment or asking for something in return, like, "Hey, I thought of you when I saw this today. I hope this helps. Talk soon."

Number five, build relationships. *Real* relationships. Building real relationships with decision-makers takes time. Remember, you've got to play the long game if you want to be successful in sales. Stop paying attention to the fake gurus' closing garbage; this is not what the top 5 percent of salespeople do, nor is it how they act. Professional selling is about the long game, and believe me, it's worth the effort. Invest the time it takes to get to know them, their needs, challenges, common problems, fears, preferences, etc. Sometimes, by *not* trying to sell them, you sell them. If you have a podcast or conduct LinkedIn Lives, invite them to be a guest. If you have an extra ticket to a game, if you see an event they should know about, if you can make a personal introduction for them, that's even better. Trust and credibility are pillars of creating real relationships, and you simply cannot rush them.

Last, number six is to become an expert. Spend the time, effort, energy, and hard work it takes to become a thought leader in your space.

The more people see you, the better. You've got to be active on LinkedIn (especially if you're in the B2B space)! Unfortunately, LinkedIn is only as good as the amount you use it, like the gym. Just having a LinkedIn profile is like having the gym key fob on your keychain. It does nothing. You have to use it! Post content frequently, at least a couple of times a week at a minimum. Post your own thoughts, share and comment on others' posts, and join LinkedIn groups. You've got to be active! Look for opportunities to conduct workshops, present at industry events, host your own webinars, and speak as a guest on as many podcasts as you can. Take the steps necessary to become an expert, thought leader, or influencer in your space. Doors won't open themselves, and this won't happen overnight.

In today's competitive business landscape, connecting with the decision-maker is crucial to your success as a sales professional. By understanding their needs, challenges, common problems, and motivations to fix those problems, you can tailor your approach and present your solution in ways that truly resonate with them. Approach each interaction with professionalism, empathy, and the desire to provide value. By doing so, you'll not only increase your chances of closing more deals, but you'll also forge long-term, mutually beneficial relationships.

The top 5 percent of salespeople do not prospect via the hit-and-hope mentality or spray-and-pray strategy in hopes of selling something. They are tactical, strategic, and precise when it comes to prospecting, and that's why they make more sales than everybody else. By defining your ICP and targeting the right decision-makers, you'll increase your closing rates, shorten your sales cycle, secure larger average deal sizes, generate more referrals, sign longer deals, increase your income, and create more consistent results.

MOTIVATING AND INSPIRING TODAY'S SALESPEOPLE

ONE OF THE BIGGEST MISTAKES sales managers continue to make is to follow the Golden Rule with their salespeople: Treat others as you would like to be treated. We've all heard it before. Heck, many of us learned from our parents to adhere to this mantra. Well, I'm about to tell you the opposite. *Don't do this, ever!*

If you're a sales leader, it is critically important that you never treat your salespeople the way *you* want to be treated. Just because *you're* motivated by hitting the company's numbers, it doesn't mean they are. Just because *you're* motivated by money, it doesn't mean they are. Just because *you* like lobster, it doesn't mean they do. Just because *you* love country music, it doesn't mean they do. The list goes on and on, and if you don't adhere to this message, it will impede your growth as a leader and demotivate your team. Instead, follow the Platinum Rule: Treat others how *they* want to be treated.

It doesn't matter whether your salespeople are extrinsically, intrinsically, or altruistically motivated as long as they are motivated. If they are unmotivated in general, it's time to find some new salespeople. If you're not motivating them according to their personal motivation style, and your company doesn't recognize that your compensation plans need to be more than purely money-driven, the impact on your sales team will be minimal. Can you imagine if there were a tool that could identify which style (extrinsic, intrinsic, or altruistic) each of your salespeople is motivated by? ☺ There is, and it's called The Sales DNA Test! Have I mentioned that yet?! Remember, leaders, if you want your salespeople to reach their full potential, you've got to motivate your sales team based on their specific individual motivational styles. Then, you'll start to see the results you're looking for.

Proper Motivation

Properly motivating your sales team can be the missing link to success in your sales organization. It's not the be-all and end-all, but it plays a very important role. Mastering the basics of motivation is critical to your success as a sales leader, and I'm going to share with you five basic strategies to help you motivate your sales team more effectively. If you're a salesperson reading this section, count how many of these strategies your sales leader implements with you. I hope it's all of them!

- Help them change their behaviors.
- Help them do more of what they're already doing.
- Help them accomplish what they won't on their own.
- Help them embrace a greater sense of urgency.
- Help them overachieve.

It definitely takes time, practice, effort, learning, implementation, and dedication to execute these strategies on a daily basis, but keep these five strategies in mind as you continue reading and jot down some ways you can begin to implement them. Following are several methods of motivation currently implemented by successful sales managers to drive production on their sales teams. You can apply these in a variety of situations.

Praise

It's amazing how people positively respond when they hear just a few encouraging words from somebody they look up to. How do you feel when people tell you how awesome you are and that you did a great job? Exactly.

Public Recognition

For some of your salespeople, there's nothing greater than being recognized in front of the team or company. Conversely, shaming someone publicly or displaying a salesperson at the bottom of the list can be emotionally devastating. Shoving your dog's nose into its own poop doesn't motivate your dog to avoid an accident on the kitchen floor; it just makes you an animal abuser.

Their Dreams

You can use *their* dreams as a motivational tool but *not your* dreams, *your* goals, or *your* quotas. Only *theirs* will work! Maybe they're motivated by achieving a specific target, crossing off a bucket list item, or making the President's Club trip. You could say things like, "Hey, Ariana, how close are you to booking that trip to Australia you've always wanted to take?"

Awards

Some salespeople are motivated by awards. Ribbons, trophies, plaques . . . They've already got a spot on their bookshelf, and they're just waiting to put that number one account opener trophy in it. We have a client with a high-performing salesperson, and all he cares about is winning the monthly contest that awards the parking space in front of the building so he doesn't have to walk through the snow!

Growth

This is often overlooked, but some salespeople are looking for growth opportunities, and they're excited about excelling and advancing through the ranks of the company. Use that to your advantage by sharing with them the opportunities for a promotion or a new role. Do not dangle a promotion or company advancement in front of them, but provide a path to those positions for high performers and share with them exactly what they need to do to get there.

Money

Some salespeople are motivated by money, but not all salespeople are. Reread that. You can structure incentive programs, give them multiple compensation plan options, and add accelerator bonuses based on sales, profitability, client retention, etc. But once again, you need to find out what *they* genuinely want. It's not about what *you* want.

There's More to Compensation than Financial Rewards

Objective Management Group (OMG), our partner and founder of The Sales DNA Test (our sales assessment), has done some extremely valuable research on money as a motivator. They discovered that the percentage of salespeople who are purely money-motivated has been decreasing year after year for the past twenty years.[1] It's not that salespeople aren't motivated by money anymore; they're just not as money-motivated as they were at the beginning of their career, when their money motivation may have helped them get to where they are today. The data show that long-term successful salespeople and brand-new salespeople don't value money the way they did twenty years ago. Both groups now seek purpose, advancement, work-life balance, and flexibility in a new career before they look for financial security.

According to OMG's thirty-plus years of data, the last couple of years show a tremendous shift in how people are motivated.[2] In 2007, about 50 percent of the sales population was extrinsically or money-motivated. Just four years later, in 2011, that percentage dropped to 27 percent.[3] It dropped by almost half. Today, the percentage of salespeople who are purely motivated by money is under 10 percent.

Contrary to what that data show us, most compensation plans and incentive programs are designed with money in mind as the sole motivating factor. But that will only inspire salespeople if they're motivated by money. According to more than three decades of scientific data, less than 10 percent of your sales team will be really excited by those incentives.

Data discovered by another amazing author I mentioned previously, Daniel Pink, show us that more salespeople are intrinsically motivated rather than extrinsically motivated. We suggest that every leader we work with reads the book *Drive* (or listens to the audiobook version). It's amazing. It's one of the best leadership books ever written, and I highly recommend it. Most companies should evaluate how their compensation plans are designed and how their incentive contests work. If you try to motivate a salesperson with money when they either have a ton of money already or couldn't care less about money, you're not exactly going to incentivize them to perform better.

I learned something about compensation through a friend of mine, Jonathan King, of System & Soul, who developed something that still sticks with me today. It's called the 6 Dimensions of Compensation, and it reveals there's a lot more to compensation than salary, commissions, and bonuses. Too often, we think about compensation strictly through a financial lens, and if we think people are staying with our companies for monetary reasons only, we're naïve at best. We all know why people leave their organizations, and thousands of studies clearly show us why. They leave due to poor management, lousy leadership, unsupportive work environments, lack of appreciation, and limited growth opportunities. The results of neglecting these extremely important aspects of developing a strong culture can be costly.

It's estimated that disengaged employees cost the world almost $8 trillion in lost productivity, and I'm guessing a big piece of that number is due to salespeople feeling disengaged. The sad part is that most C-suite executives still don't seem to understand this, and they think throwing money at people and improving compensation plans for their salespeople will do the trick. It won't. If you really want to improve the performance of your sales team and create a culture in which your people can thrive, here are the six forms of compensation your team either needs or wants. And if you're not providing it to them, they'll find it somewhere else.

6 DIMENSIONS OF COMPENSATION

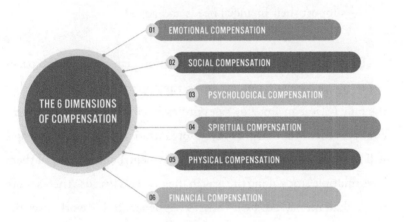

THE 6 DIMENSIONS OF COMPENSATION

01 EMOTIONAL COMPENSATION
02 SOCIAL COMPENSATION
03 PSYCHOLOGICAL COMPENSATION
04 SPIRITUAL COMPENSATION
05 PHYSICAL COMPENSATION
06 FINANCIAL COMPENSATION

1. **EMOTIONAL COMPENSATION:** Do your salespeople enjoy their work, and do they feel supported at all times?

2. **SOCIAL COMPENSATION:** Do your salespeople like the people they work with? Do they have a sense of community and trust with their peers and you?

3. **PSYCHOLOGICAL COMPENSATION:** Do your salespeople have opportunities to grow personally and professionally in your organization?

4. **SPIRITUAL COMPENSATION:** Do your salespeople have meaning and purpose in what they do every day? Is it more than just
the latest sales job for them?

5. **PHYSICAL COMPENSATION:** Do your salespeople have flexibility in their day-to-day work? Are their personal needs met,
and are their boundaries respected?

6. **FINANCIAL COMPENSATION:** Do your salespeople feel com-
pensated appropriately for their work? Does the compensation
support their financial needs and goals?

Do you need an attractive compensation plan and financial pack-
age to incentivize and potentially recruit top performers? Yes. Is that
the only reason an amazing sales professional will leave their current
employer and come to work for your organization? No. Top salespeople
will never have a hard time finding employment, but too many of them
have multiple stops along the way in their careers because there's more
to life than money. And with what's happened in this world over the
past few years, more and more companies are beginning to realize that
their salespeople might be right.

Three Styles of Motivation

As we just learned, not all salespeople are motivated by money alone.
Some are, but most aren't. Knowing this to be true, you need to focus
your attention on identifying the specific motivations of each of your
salespeople. Once you determine their motivation style, you'll be
shocked by how much more effective you are as a leader. (Ahem, The
Sales DNA Test can help. . . .)

There are three main styles of motivation for salespeople. Extrinsic motivation is based on money, rewards, toys, awards, and other material things. Intrinsic motivation is based on recognition, fulfillment, joy, satisfaction, and mastery. Altruistic motivation is based on helping others first for the greater good, like putting the customers' needs ahead of one's own. Weird, huh? Surprisingly, the data show that intrinsically motivated people will generally outperform extrinsically motivated people over the long term. Although extrinsic motivation works better in the short term to get instant results. Let's dive into the details of each style.

External Rewards

Think about your motivation (as a salesperson, sales manager, or leader). Are you reading this book to make more money or get a promotion? If so, that means you're looking to gain external reinforcement, so you are extrinsically motivated. Extrinsic motivation is usually defined as our tendency to engage in activities to achieve some external reward. It's important to know that these rewards can be either tangible or psychological. Money and trophies are two common examples of tangible rewards. People engage in activities they might not otherwise find enjoyable or rewarding in order to receive something. Athletes engage in extremely strenuous and difficult training sessions in order to compete in sporting events to win trophies and awards, like the Super Bowl or the World Cup.

Some forms of extrinsic motivation include praise and public acclaim. A child might clean his room to receive praise from his mom and dad. An actor might perform in a role to win an Oscar. In both examples, it's still a type of motivating reward that's external to the actual process of participating in the event, which means they are rewarding for extrinsically motivated people.

Offering rewards can increase motivation in some salespeople, but that's not always the case. In fact, offering too many rewards can lead to a decrease in the performance of intrinsically motivated salespeople. If your motivation techniques are solely based on extrinsically motivated salespeople, but you have intrinsically motivated salespeople on your team, you're going to do more damage than good. Extrinsic motivators are best applied in situations where salespeople have very little interest in performing an activity. You want to make sure you incentivize that activity by using a specific tool.

For example, if a salesperson hates cold calling and they are extrinsically motivated, you could say, "Make a hundred dials, and you get fifty bucks." Now, they may be motivated by that particular incentive and much more likely to make those cold calls. I'm excited to teach you more about the *cost of inaction* in a later chapter, which would reframe this example to have the sales manager say, "You don't have to make the hundred dials, but if you don't, here's what that leads to . . ." Extrinsic motivation generally works for short-term tasks, not for long-term growth and achievement.

Extrinsic motivation is not a bad thing. External rewards can be a very useful and effective tool for getting your salespeople motivated and getting them to perform a task. This can be particularly important when salespeople need to complete something they find difficult or uninteresting, such as entering information into their CRM, giving you their pipeline reports, making cold calls, etc. You just need to know who's motivated by what and use those tools accordingly.

Internal Rewards

Don't "show me the money!" I'm hoping you heard Jerry Maguire shouting that out loud right now, and if you have no idea who Jerry Maguire is, just google "show me the money!"[4] With that in mind, I'll say it again: It's not always about the money. Some sales managers still can't wrap their heads around the fact that there's more to life than money. Hard to believe, isn't it? Sometimes, people want to live a joyful, happy, and fulfilling life, and they realize they can't take the money with them. Intrinsic motivation refers to behavior that's driven by internal rewards. In other words, the motivation to engage in a behavior arises from within the individual because it's naturally satisfying for them.

My favorite activity in the world—the one that makes me happiest—is fishing. I can be on the water all day long, not catch a damn thing, and have an amazing day. For you, maybe it's gardening, painting, reading, dancing, or playing golf that makes you happy and gives you joy. These activities may or may not produce something tangible for you, but you do them because you derive pleasure from them. When you pursue an activity purely for the enjoyment of it, you're doing so because you're intrinsically motivated.

That isn't to say that intrinsically motivated behaviors don't come with their own rewards. Certain activities can generate amazing feelings when they give people a sense of meaning, like volunteering and helping at community events. These activities may give you a sense of progress when you see your hard work accomplishing something positive, like supporting a community organization with a fundraiser or completing a household project. Or maybe your intrinsic motivation comes from performing a new skill or becoming more efficient at a particular task, like playing a new song on guitar or breaking eighty in golf. In general, people are more creative when they're intrinsically motivated. So, in work settings, if you're doing something that you find rewarding, interesting, and challenging, you're more likely to produce new ideas and creative solutions to those problems.

Intrinsically motivated salespeople want to master their craft. They love what they do, they want to achieve mastery, and they want to feel like they're doing a great job. Intrinsically motivated salespeople usually welcome coaching and support because they want to improve every day. They are not motivated by money, and if you try to motivate them with money, you're going to cause more harm than good. You've got to motivate your salespeople the way *they* want to be motivated, not the way *you* want to be motivated. Remember the Platinum Rule.

Altruistic Rewards

The third form of motivation is altruistic. Of the three styles of motivation, this one appears to be growing most among today's professional salespeople. I know this may sound strange, but there are some salespeople who actually care about their customers, clients, coworkers, and company's needs more than they care about their own needs. And even though this is the least common form of motivation and the style that's least present in salespeople, it doesn't mean that it's nonexistent.

What inspires these "crazy" salespeople to give their time, energy, effort, and money for the betterment of others, even when they receive nothing tangible in return? Well, these are the altruistically motivated salespeople. Altruism is unselfish concern for other people. It means doing things simply out of a desire to help someone without a sense of obligation or self-serving purpose. Everyday life is filled with small acts of altruism—everything from the guy at the grocery store who holds the door open for you to the woman who gives twenty bucks to the homeless man on the corner. News stories often focus on grander cases of altruism, like the guy who runs into an icy river to rescue a drowning dog or a selfless donor who gives millions of dollars to charity.

You may be familiar with altruism, but many leaders have difficulty grasping the concept that it can be present in salespeople. Why would a salesperson not care about making a sale or lining their own pockets? Do they enjoy helping others for truly altruistic reasons, or are there hidden benefits for them that guide their altruistic behaviors? Some psychologists believe that while people often behave altruistically for selfish reasons, true altruism is not only possible but prevalent. Other psychologists have instead suggested that empathy for others is often guided by the desire to help oneself. Whatever the reasons behind it, our world would be a much sadder place without altruism, and believe it or not, you may have someone on your sales team who is altruistically motivated.

What Might Work for Your Team?

Learning what motivates your salespeople as individuals will determine your ultimate success as a leader. That's why The Sales DNA Test is so important—we show you exactly which style of motivation your salespeople have and the degree to which they are motivated by each style. Wouldn't it be helpful to know which of your salespeople are extrinsically motivated versus intrinsically motivated and which ones are altruistic or may have a combination of two or more styles? Wouldn't you like to know whether people respond better to being pushed or respond better to pushing themselves? Wouldn't you want to know whether people perform better when they're closely managed or when they're completely left alone? Wouldn't it be helpful for you to know whether money is a motivator or a nonfactor? Wouldn't you want to know who performs better when competing against others and who performs better when competing against their own expectations?

This is precisely why The Sales DNA Test is crucial and why we insist we test every salesperson on the team before we start working with any client. How could we know how to help, guide, suggest, or give a recommendation if we didn't know all the ins and outs of the sales team we're trying to help?

What if a mediocre salesperson could rise to another level of production if the compensation plan and rewards were compelling enough? Wouldn't you want to know who responds better to public recognition or private praise? For some salespeople, it doesn't get any better than hearing their name called out, receiving an award or a plaque, or seeing themselves listed in your company newsletter. But other salespeople couldn't care less about all that because they get satisfaction from knowing that they're one of the best salespeople on the team and their clients love them. These are the things that are important for you to understand if you want to become a great leader. Understanding how to motivate the individuals on your sales team is critical. And if you can master this aspect of sales leadership, your team, and your company, will achieve results you never thought possible.

Look for Thirsty Horses

Some of you read that heading and became really excited because you love all things horses, and this majestic animal provides us with so many great analogies, metaphors, and similes for many aspects of life! You may not know a thing about horses, but I'm going to ask a question that you'll probably know the answer to. What happens if you try to pull a horse that doesn't want to move? Well, if you guessed any of the following, you'd be right.

Resistance

The horse may resist your efforts by planting its feet and refusing to budge. Horses are strong animals, and if they choose not to move, it can be challenging to force them.

Backing Up

In some cases, instead of moving forward, a horse may choose to back up when pressured. This can be dangerous if you're standing behind the horse, as it may inadvertently step on you.

Reactivity

If the horse feels threatened or stressed by your attempts to pull it, it may react with fear or aggression. This can include rearing, kicking, or biting, which can be dangerous for you.

Reaction to Stress and Fear

Repeated attempts to force a horse to move can lead to increased stress and fear in the horse. This can negatively impact the horse's trust and relationship with you.

Training Issues

For trained horses, repeatedly forcing them to move when they don't want to can erode their training and make them less responsive to cues in the future. It can also make them less willing to work with you.

Hmmm, have you figured out the analogy between salespeople and horses yet? Guess what happens when you try to pull a salesperson, especially the wrong one. You now know the answer. You've also heard the phrase, "You can lead a horse to water, but you can't make it drink." This is true because you can't want something for someone more than they want it for themselves. I use a similar phrase when it comes to leading salespeople: look for thirsty horses. If your horse is already thirsty, there's no pulling, prodding, poking, or hoping. There's no resistance, no digging of its heels, no added stress, no fear, and certainly no pain. There's nothing you have to do other than calmly lead him to water, which is where he already wants to go.

The challenge for most sales leaders is finding thirsty horses. I'm sure at some point in your life as a sales manager, you've tried to get your people to do what you wanted them to do: make more calls, use the CRM, file their reports, role-play, etc. You bang your head against the wall because you can't seem to figure out why they won't do it! Well, guess what? You've got the wrong horses.

In the restaurant business, you must start with high-quality ingredients if you want to make amazing dishes and have your customers rave about the quality of your food. In the business world, especially in sales hiring, you must start with the *right* candidates if you want to build a high-performing sales team. In other words, look to hire salespeople who are already internally motivated, who have the desire to become world-class salespeople, who have the will to win, who have a work ethic and commitment that are unmatched, and who have the skills and mindset necessary for success.

Believe it or not, there's a way to discover all these things *before* hiring a salesperson. It's something called the Will to Sell, and it's part of The Sales DNA Test. The test measures these very important parameters to let you know whether you have a thirsty horse or a salesperson you'll have to prod, poke, and pull. This is an assessment our clients use for every single candidate they even consider hiring. Without this tool, they'd just be guessing. Companies that use The Sales DNA Test to evaluate sales candidates before they ever set eyes on them or speak to them have a 72 percent chance of hiring a top-half performer.

THE POWER OF SALES DNA

ASSESSMENTS AND ASSUMPTIONS ARE LIKE OIL AND WATER—
they don't go together. The Red Sox and Yankees, Michigan and Ohio
State, and sardines and ice cream are just a few other things that are
opposed to having harmonious relationships with one another. One
of my favorite mantras applies here as well: "When you assume, you
make an a** out of you and an a** out of me."

Assessments have been around for more than one hundred years.
History shows us that personality testing began with Woodworth's
Personal Data Sheet in 1917.[1] That test was developed to identify
soldiers prone to nervous breakdowns during enemy bombardment
in World War I. The army was trying to predict whether certain people would be prone to shell shock. Another famous assessment, the
Myers-Briggs Type Indicator, also started around the same time. It was
created based on the assumption that people have preferred modes of
perception (sensing or intuition) and judgment (thinking or feeling),
as well as attitudes that lead to extroversion or introversion, which
affect how they judge or perceive the outside world. This assessment
then categorized people into different personality types.

Countless experts and psychologists argue that categories and personality types don't predict individual or team effectiveness. Studies have also found that more than half the people who retake this particular personality assessment get a different result the second time. (One such study includes "Personality Stability from Age 14 to Age 77 Years" in the National Library of Medicine.[2]) Even with that knowledge, the test is still used today, and many others are based on the same principles.

Guess what assessments were *not* created for. To determine someone's effectiveness in sales or sales leadership! In the world of business, effective talent acquisition is a vital component of success. It's no secret that recruiting, hiring, and retaining the right people can make all the difference in achieving and surpassing your company's goals. And more important, if you want to continue to drive revenue, grow and scale your company, and increase profitability, it's essential to build, develop, and lead a high-performing sales team.

One of the best and most effective ways to accomplish that is to assess candidates you're considering for new sales positions accurately and evaluate your current sales team. Therein lies the problem. What assessment should you use? Determining which assessment will accurately predict a salesperson's success has been an ongoing debate for decades. More than two thousand assessments are available in the marketplace today, and it can be incredibly overwhelming to figure out which ones to use. In most cases, companies struggle to determine which type of assessment is better—personality- or skills-based.

Unfortunately, most assessments used today are based on assumptions, and you know what happens when you do that. Assessments are used in two contexts: evaluating current employees and candidates for employment. Based on what you're attempting to measure, one assessment could be helpful for evaluating existing employees but, at the same time, be completely irrelevant for evaluating potential employees. There are too many factors to list that illustrate the differences between the two categories; however, it's probably a good business practice to evaluate an investment *before you invest* rather than try to analyze why you lost all your money after you invested.

I don't blame companies for using assessments in the hiring process so they can decipher whether a candidate is truly the person they present in their interview or actually a fabricated, ideal candidate avatar refined with practice and artificial intelligence to hoodwink you into hiring them. For this reason and many others, the success rate for US companies when hiring salespeople hovers around 25 percent. This means that for every ten sales hires a company makes, only two become above-average performers. One out of four! Companies know this to be true and are increasingly counting on prehire assessments to help them better predict the future success of new sales hires.

Most assessments in the marketplace are used for evaluating behaviors, deciphering communication styles, and checking for cultural fits. They have *absolutely nothing* to do with evaluating someone's ability to sell your specific product or service. All the well-known assessments can be helpful *after* you hire someone to see whether they fit in well with the team, understand how best to manage them, identify their communication style, and learn about a plethora of other traits. Nevertheless, generic personality assessments *should never be used* to determine current or future success in sales. Even more confusing is that assessments fall into four main categories: personality, behavioral, aptitude, and psychological. As you can probably guess, the only one remotely applicable to salespeople would be a sales aptitude assessment. The other three have absolutely nothing to do with selling, nor could they ever attempt to predict success in sales accurately. They're not built for that—they weren't created for that, and they don't measure the traits necessary to do that.

The Downsides of Most Assessments

Assessments can provide valuable insights into an individual's characteristics and abilities, but there are numerous reasons why these insights should not be applied in the context of evaluating salespeople.

All Sales Roles Aren't Created Equal

Sales roles vary in countless ways. Is it an inside sales role or an outside sales role? Are you looking for a hunter or a farmer? Is there a short or long sales cycle? Is it a widget, a complex product/service, or a conceptual sale? Does the product/service cost $200 or $200K? Does it require the salesperson to have strong negotiation skills? Is it B2B or B2C? Will they face tremendous amounts of competition, or are they the only game in town? As you well know, sales positions vary tremendously and often require a very specific set of diverse skills, qualities, and requirements. Assessments that focus solely on personality traits, behaviors, or aptitude shouldn't claim they can predict success in specific sales roles with this amount of differentiation.

Predictive Validity Is Low or Nonexistent

As you'll soon learn, the research conducted by OMG on the predictive validity of assessments for sales roles has yielded mixed results at best. Most of the studies conducted have found no correlation between certain personality traits and sales performance, nor have they found some magic benchmark of behaviors that fits every salesperson. Success in sales has nothing to do with skills, strengths, or behaviors; success will only come when a salesperson can execute what's needed at the time it's needed.

Stereotyping and Relying on Biases Won't Help You

Using the wrong assessments for hiring salespeople can lead to stereotyping and relying on patently false biases. The assumption that extroverts are better at sales or that certain personality traits are universally predictive of success in sales is misleading at best. The success or failure of a salesperson in your organization depends on a multitude of factors. Making broad generalizations based on the assumptions of personality assessments will not only lead to biased hiring decisions but will also lead to bad hire after bad hire.

Ignoring the Value of Soft Skills

While assessments may identify behaviors, cognitive aptitudes, and personality traits, most do not adequately assess soft skills like listening, empathy, adaptability, curiosity, conscientiousness, and problem-solving. Such qualities are essential for building customer relationships, navigating complex sales situations, and creating more opportunities consistently, which lead to long-term success in sales.

It Will Cost You Millions of Dollars

The average company makes the right sales hire only about 25 percent of the time. And to make things even worse, the average bad sales hire will cost a company $1.3M in lost revenue.[3] But if it's so costly, why do companies keep making the same mistakes? Because they use the wrong assessments based on the wrong assumptions and end up hiring the wrong salespeople!

Using the proper assessment with your organization does matter, but it's also important to realize you can't rely solely on assessments during the hiring process. We suggest that our clients combine assessments with other evaluation methods like interviews, role-play exercises, homework assignments, background checks, and various other techniques to form a more comprehensive view of a candidate's potential for success in a specific sales role.

Assessments: The Breakdown

Unfortunately, many of the assessments that companies use today (and they're paying a ton of money to use them) have the same predictive validity as shaking up a Magic 8 Ball. Imagine there was an assessment specifically built for sales professionals that was 50 percent predictive of future sales success. Would you consider using it? What if I told you there was an assessment that's more than 70 percent predictive of identifying top-half salespeople, and 100 percent predictive of identifying bottom-half performers? Would you consider using it? If so, pay close attention when we dive into The Sales DNA Test later in this chapter. As I mentioned, companies are using four main assessments as tools to evaluate candidates and current employees. Personality, behavioral, psychological, and aptitude assessments are used in several industries, such as the medical field, higher education, the public sector, and the private sector, to gather information about individuals in different ways. Let's break them down and look at each one closely.

Personality Assessments

Personality assessments aim to measure an individual's personality traits, characteristics, and behaviors. They seek to understand a person's typical patterns of thinking, feeling, and behaving. These assessments often use self-reported questionnaires, interviews, or behavioral observations to gather information about a person's personality. These assessments are *not* sales-role specific, and the questions are asked in a social context, not in a selling context, which makes them inconsequential and certainly not applicable to a selling environment. As a result, personality assessments are not in any way predictive of success in sales and are ineffective as a sales development or coaching tool.

Behavioral Assessments

Behavioral assessments aim to measure an individual's behavior in specific contexts. They are used to understand behavior patterns and identify potential issues or areas for improvement. Behavioral assessments typically involve direct observation, checklists, and recording of behaviors. They can also use self-reporting to gather information about an individual's behaviors. The questions are also typically asked in a social context and not a selling context, which makes them inconsequential to assessing salespeople and inapplicable to a selling environment. How someone behaves in a social setting does not necessarily predict how they'll behave in a sales setting. Therefore, these assessments are also not in any way predictive of success in sales and thus ineffective as a sales development or coaching tool.

Psychological Assessments

Psychological assessments are typically used by psychologists and other mental health professionals to evaluate an individual's mental and emotional well-being, cognitive functioning, and psychological characteristics. Psychological assessments can include interviews, standardized tests, questionnaires, and clinical observations. They are used to diagnose and treat mental health disorders, assess cognitive abilities, and understand emotional and behavioral functioning. Once again, these types of assessments are not predictive of success in sales, and they are ineffective as a sales development or coaching tool.

Aptitude Assessments

Aptitude assessments aim to measure an individual's potential or ability to acquire specific skills or knowledge in the future. They help predict how well someone might perform in certain tasks or professions. Aptitude assessments often involve standardized tests or assessments that evaluate cognitive abilities, such as problem-solving, reasoning, and critical thinking. The SATs and GREs are aptitude assessments commonly used for college admissions. Unsurprisingly, they should never be used to determine future sales success!

These four types of assessments each serve a unique purpose, and they can be helpful in some cases. They can be applied in various contexts to gain insights into different aspects of individuals' personalities, behaviors, abilities, and psychological well-being. The challenge lies within the details that do not always appear on the surface. Are they accurate? Do they work? Can I trust the data?

Ethical factors, predictive validity, and reliability are crucial factors to consider when using and interpreting the data collected from any of these assessment categories.

Many assessments today are marketed by their various companies as sales assessments, but the only thing about them that is sales-specific is the language used in their marketing materials.

Predictive Validity

Predictive validity is a concept used to measure the extent to which the results of a test or assessment can predict future performance or outcomes. In other words, it assesses the ability of a test to accurately forecast an individual's future behavior or success in a particular area based on their scores or performance on that test. To determine the predictive validity of an assessment, researchers typically collect data from individuals who have taken the test and then observe their performance or outcomes in the relevant domain over a defined period. The correlation between assessment scores and actual performance or outcomes is then calculated. The strength of this correlation indicates the predictive validity of the assessment.

How well does a Tarot card reading predict someone's future? How predictive is reading someone's horoscope? How prognostic is reading someone's palm? There's a difference between fun and kitschy vs. scientifically proven and predictively valid. My guess would be that most companies would not want to put their future success into the hands of fun and kitschy. If you are seriously considering (or currently using) assessments in your business, and you want to make sure you're not wasting thousands of dollars on testing and trusting inaccurate data, please ask your assessment provider for their technical manual. The strength of predictive validity depends on the specific context and the goals of the assessment. There is no fixed threshold or magic number that determines whether an assessment has high or acceptable predictive validity; it varies from one assessment to another and depends on the criteria being predicted.

Many behavioral assessments simply take data from a small pool of people, compare the behaviors of those people, and then see what specific behaviors are present among the top performers in the pool. The first problem is that the sample size is usually way too small. Second, they don't look at the bottom performers, but often, they have almost the same behaviors as the top performers. They do not account for how these people deal with negativity, adversity, objections, selling situations, etc. Many aptitude tests assume that because you know how to do something, you can execute it effectively. This is simply untrue. If you spent a day with Arnold Schwarzenegger and he showed you everything he did to become Mr. Olympia, do you think you'd be able to do it too? You may have the aptitude, capacity, and knowledge to *know what to do*, but you probably couldn't execute it. This is yet another reason why these assessments are very poor predictors of future sales success. Behavior does not predict sales success. Aptitude does not predict sales success. Personality does not predict sales success. *Period.*

The Power of Sales DNA

I cannot begin to tell you how impactful The Sales DNA Test has been for me, personally and professionally. This is precisely why The Sales DNA Test is the only assessment we use with our clients, and the entire foundation of our company is based on it. It's the only assessment that's built for salespeople, by salespeople, and verified by a third party. It's the only assessment on the planet that specifically measures the competencies that matter in today's world of professional selling. This is not a generic personality test that provides no meaningful data to help you drive sales. There's a Sales DNA Test for salespeople, sales managers, and sales executives, and they all have completely different metrics and measurements related to those specific roles.

Well, things have changed. With the economic climate we're in today (and in which we'll probably remain for the next few lean years), if you don't pivot, recalibrate, and learn how to sell to today's consumers in this unique marketplace, you're going to be left in the dust. And if you can't identify the traits and skills necessary to succeed in sales at your particular company or in your particular role, what exactly are you relying on to ensure success? The challenge is that most assessments, as we just learned, simply will not and cannot accurately predict sales performance. Almost every assessment out there evaluates the person; The Sales DNA Test evaluates the *salesperson inside the person*. Can they perform in sales? Can they lead sales teams effectively? That's what matters! If they can't do those things, who cares about their behaviors, strengths, or personality type?!

As you know, there are thousands of assessments to choose from. Some tell you what acronym you are, some tell you what type of personality you have, some measure your IQ, some tell you what color you are, and some may even tell you what kind of dinosaur you are. And somehow, they're supposed to predict your success in sales?!

There is one, and only one, assessment I've ever seen that can accurately predict sales ability and success, and that's The Sales DNA Test. Built by OMG four decades ago, it's a sales-specific competency- and mindset-based assessment that has helped three million sales professionals in forty thousand companies evaluate potential candidates for hire and pinpoint why their existing sales teams haven't reached their full potential.

OMG was founded by Dave Kurlan, who is renowned for his ground-breaking work in evaluating salespeople and sales organizations and has written several books and white papers on the subject. He also happens to be in the Sales Hall of Fame! OMG was built by experts on sales, sales leadership, selling, sales processes, sales challenges, sales strategy, and sales tactics. It's very difficult to measure what you don't know, and it's even more difficult to predict future performance when you don't understand how specific findings can impact a sales process that's also impacted by external sales challenges and expectations. OMG's assessment (which we call The Sales DNA Test) was built from the ground up—*with the sole intention of purposely creating an assessment for sales.* Most assessments were built for some other reason (to evaluate personality, behavior, culture, leadership, and aptitude) and then jammed into a selling context. The Sales DNA Test isn't a generic assessment that's been "modified" for sales to appear sales specific. Some assessment companies are still using data and publishing guidelines from fifty years ago. Before OMG was founded, companies weren't even considering using assessments to evaluate their sales teams. OMG is the pioneer in this space, and they continue to provide the only sales-specific, role-specific, predictively valid assessment in the marketplace today.

The Sales DNA Test does not look at someone's personality traits, behavioral style, or psychological makeup. It does have a component that reveals sales aptitude, but the emphasis is on whether an individual will *execute the skills they have* and *which weaknesses will prevent execution*. More importantly, an even greater emphasis is placed on whether a candidate or current salesperson will succeed in a specific sales position for a particular company in a specific industry working in their target market. It is the single most valuable tool I've seen in my almost thirty years in this profession.

When it's used to evaluate existing salespeople and sales leaders, the primary purpose of The Sales DNA Test is to provide additional insights and knowledge about a salesperson or sales manager that you would never have known otherwise. The point is to help someone become more effective in all aspects of selling or sales leadership, even though they may be great at many of them already. The Sales DNA Test is not intended to be critical or negative in any way; the purpose behind it is to help people answer the following three questions:

- Am I selling (or leading my sales team) in the best way possible?

- Are there important skills or beliefs I haven't yet developed or mastered?

- Are there weaknesses preventing me from being as effective as I can be?

The test has nothing to do with how great you are in sales now or how great you may have been in the past. Its purpose is to show you how much better you *could* be in your role as a salesperson or a sales manager if you implement some suggested improvements. Remember, this isn't a typical culture-based assessment or personality profile. The findings will help you see the ways you think and act that are affecting your performance as a salesperson or sales manager.

You learned about the power of predictive validity in the last section, so let's return to that for a minute. OMG uses the most time-consuming and expensive form of validation. Unlike simpler methods of validation, *predictive validity requires a connection to on-the-job performance.* The challenge is that OMG's predictive validity is so high some people can't believe it, so they want to revalidate it themselves. Validation is an expensive and time-consuming process, and you'll find that most personality or behavioral assessments don't use predictive validity because there simply isn't a correlation between their findings and on-the-job performance. Most want to avoid the subject, deflect the science, and distract their customers from the fact that their assessment is about as predictively valid as shaking up a Magic 8 Ball. As you know by now, most of the traits, styles, behaviors, and categories that are measured by traditional assessment companies are measured only in a *social* or *life* context, but The Sales DNA Test's findings are measured only in a sales or sales leadership context.

As I mentioned previously, the success rate for US companies when hiring salespeople hovers around 25 percent. When The Sales DNA Test is used for hiring salespeople, OMG's predictive validity is over 70 percent!

The Will to Sell

OMG—our amazing and incredible partner—has evaluated roughly three million salespeople over the past four decades and developed The Sales DNA Test to help companies better assess their existing sales teams and screen candidates for new sales and sales leadership positions. The Sales DNA Test measures twenty-one specific competencies in a salesperson (and twenty specific competencies in a sales manager). If you don't know your own hindrances when it comes to sales (or sales leadership), and if you don't know your own self-limiting beliefs, how on Earth can you fix them?

One of the most important metrics developed by OMG is called the Will to Sell. This specific competency in a salesperson comprises five distinct attributes that ultimately determine whether someone is likely to become a world-class sales professional. The five attributes are desire, commitment, outlook, motivation, and responsibility. Following is a brief breakdown of each competency and how it impacts the success of a salesperson, both positively and negatively.

Desire measures a salesperson's drive, determination, and internal will to become a world-class sales professional. When this scores high as a strength, salespeople feel the urgency to take action, run through brick walls, or make those extra calls, and they care deeply about becoming great in sales. When this scores low as a weakness in a salesperson, they focus on the non-sales-related activities like organizing their CRM and alphabetizing their prospect list, they lack urgency and a passion for selling, and they don't care if they become great in sales. It is incredibly difficult to motivate salespeople who lack the desire (or no longer have the drive they once had) necessary to achieve greatness in sales.

Commitment is next, and this one's quite important. If a salesperson's commitment scores high as a strength, they tend to persevere in difficult situations, do what makes them uncomfortable, and follow through on what they say they'll do, even if they don't feel like it, which bodes well for their future success in sales. When this scores low as a weakness, it means the salesperson avoids doing anything that makes them uncomfortable in sales. Many salespeople are uncomfortable prospecting, cold calling, presenting in public, asking for referrals, and asking for the sale. And if you're not comfortable doing those things in sales, you'll avoid doing them at almost any cost, and there's very little chance you'll become a top performer.

Outlook is next on the list. If you don't have a positive attitude and outlook on life, especially as a sales professional, it's going to be tough sledding for you. The woe-is-me people, the Eeyores, and the Murphy's Law practitioners aren't typically successful in life. When outlook scores high as a strength, salespeople are positive, focused, and appreciative of where they are in their careers. They see the glass as half-full. They tend to find the silver lining in most situations, which helps them overcome adversity more frequently and leads to more success in sales. When outlook scores low as a weakness, salespeople tend to get frustrated or easily distracted by a challenge, which leads to demotivation and a lack of urgency. They tend to consider the glass half-empty, which leads them to make excuses, show attitude issues, have chips on their shoulders, complain about everything, show a disregard for policies and requests, maintain a low self-image, and have unrealistic expectations. These issues will negatively affect their performance as a salesperson, and it's not conducive to future success in just about any endeavor.

Next is motivation. When this scores high as a strength, the salesperson tends to be that "thirsty horse" we're looking for, and they're internally motivated to achieve success. If their motivation scores low as a weakness, they may be unmotivated because of the work environment they're in, may not fully believe in what they're selling, or may not be getting the support they need or the results they expect. But I think the most valuable measurement of motivation is its ability to tell you exactly what motivation style drives the salesperson. It will show exactly what percentage they're driven extrinsically, intrinsically, and altruistically. If you're a leader of salespeople and you don't know which style they're driven by, how can you properly lead them?

The last component of the Will to Sell is responsibility. If a salesperson scores high in responsibility as a strength, they tend to hold themselves accountable and take full responsibility for their results, even if the results are not good. If a salesperson receives a low responsibility score, they tend to blame only external factors for their lack of success instead of taking personal responsibility for their results. They'll blame the product, their sales manager, the competition, the pricing model, the economy, the president, the weather, and everything under the sun except the person in the mirror! Please remember, this is only one small part of what we measure on The Sales DNA Test, but if a salesperson doesn't have a strong Will to Sell, it will be almost impossible for them to become a top performer in sales.

Sales DNA Competencies

Part of The Sales DNA Test includes something called Sales DNA Competencies, which are six specific traits that determine a salesperson's ability to execute in front of their prospects. And is there anything more important for a salesperson to do besides execute when it matters? These competencies describe how a salesperson thinks, acts, behaves, believes, and executes when they're in front of prospects.

Sales skills are not the only factors that determine someone's sales capabilities. The overall level of their Sales DNA is just as important. When someone's Sales DNA is strong, a salesperson can effectively execute under pressure. They can handle complicated deals, high-dollar opportunities, ornery prospects, difficult negotiations, and stressful situations. When Sales DNA is weak, it hinders a salesperson's ability to execute under pressure. They struggle with complicated deals, can't convert high-dollar opportunities, succumb to ornery prospects, crumble during difficult negotiations, and fold in stressful situations. Six competencies make up Sales DNA: the need to be liked, staying in the moment, supportive beliefs, supportive buy cycle, comfortable discussing money, and recovery from rejection. We'll look at two of these in depth because they are, in my opinion, the most important.

Doesn't Need Approval (Also Known as the Need to Be Liked)

The first competency of Sales DNA is called *doesn't need approval*; in plain language, it's known as *the need to be liked*. The need to be liked is a serious hindrance for most adults, let alone most salespeople, and it's incredibly destructive to future success. It specifically refers to the need for a salesperson to be liked by their prospect. More than 80 percent of salespeople need to be liked by their prospects![4]

Let's begin by sharing what causes people to need to be liked by others and why this is devastating for a salesperson. It starts in childhood, unfortunately. I will never give advice to others about two things—marriage and parenting. But I do know what causes the need to be liked in most adults. (For context, how many people on TikTok or Instagram need to be liked? Probably 100 percent.) The root cause of people needing to be liked by everyone, in my humble opinion, is rooted in entitlement. I don't think people ever intend to become entitled. There's no definitive way to say someone is entitled—it's more of an interpretation or impression.

Nevertheless, it's not exactly looked upon as a redeeming quality. I'm sure there are countless studies on this topic, and I'm sure you have your own life experiences in this area as well. But I can assure you, if kids keep getting trophies for finishing in 947th place, the need to be liked will start to fester. Moreover, the expanding influence of social media only intensifies people's constant need to be liked by their followers, and this unbecoming trait will be exacerbated to the fiftieth degree.

Another factor that leads to the growth of needing to be liked is tied to the number one fear in America. More than 70 percent of adults have this fear. Do you know what it is? Public speaking is the number one fear in America! Do you know what the number two fear is? Death. Yep, death scored second! The fact that you will be dead, gone, worm food, compost, whatever you want to call it, is number two behind public speaking! *Seinfeld* has the greatest take on this I've ever heard, which can be boiled down to this: More people are afraid of giving a eulogy than being in the casket![5]

It's true, sadly. Think about someone who's deathly afraid of public speaking, singing karaoke, or being in front of a crowd. You may be thinking of yourself, and that's okay; you're in the majority! Think about that person for a second, and if it's you, think long and hard about this. What is the root cause of the fear of public speaking? It's the need to be liked. Most people are afraid of public speaking because they are mortified by the thought of looking stupid, being embarrassed, and making a fool of themselves. What drives these feelings and emotions? Caring what strangers think about you! And please, pay close attention to what I'm about to say.

The second you stop caring what strangers think about you is the second you'll start living your life for real. Hard stop.

This fear rears its ugly head in many aspects of sales, but it is particularly significant when a salesperson needs to challenge a prospect. Think about the last time a scenario required you to ask a prospect a really tough question, one that would have made them recoil a bit, so you decided not to ask it. You could also think about the last time a leadership scenario called for you to say something that would challenge your salesperson's thinking, so you chose not to say anything. It wasn't because choosing not to ask or challenge someone is a better strategy or a better tactic; it's because you didn't want to say or do anything that would hurt your chances of making the sale or lose face. You didn't want to ask a tough question that might jeopardize the way a prospect or salesperson felt about you. You wanted them to like you. That is why the need to be liked will kill you in sales and leadership. If you're a teacher, the need to be liked will affect your ability to teach. If you're a coach, the need to be liked will affect your ability to coach. If you're a leader, the need to be liked will affect your ability to lead.

When the need for approval, or as we call it, the need to be liked, scores low (meaning they DO need to be liked), it prevents the salesperson from asking challenging questions or constructively confronting prospects because they fear the prospect won't like them anymore. In their mind, this will ruin their chances of making the sale. In sales, there are plenty of times when salespeople need to push back, question, challenge, or confront a prospect, and if they have the need to be liked, they simply won't do it because they don't want the prospect not to like them. That's a problem costing salespeople millions in lifetime income. You're not going to be everybody's cup of tea. That's life.

If you really want to overcome your need to be liked, you need to focus on earning something from your prospects that's ten times as valuable as likability. Respect. You do this by demonstrating your knowledge, your passion, your experience, your honesty, and your value. The top ten percenters in sales understand that they'd rather have a client's respect than their undying love. But they are still likable! Don't get it twisted. You still need to be *likable* when you're selling, but you cannot *need* to be liked—that's the distinction.

One way for salespeople to overcome their need to be liked is to ask poignant, relevant, and challenging questions. If you ask more of the how and why questions, it encourages your prospects to share more information with you. The more information they share, the better your chances of helping them. Salespeople should also be more curious and more intentional about talking less. These tips and strategies will help you maintain more control over the sales presentation and encourage your prospects to respect you, not like you.

Comfortable Discussing Money

The second Sales DNA hindrance that has a major negative impact on the success of a salesperson is being uncomfortable discussing money. Do you know that 60 percent of salespeople are uncomfortable discussing money? That's like saying 60 percent of dentists are uncomfortable working on teeth. Or 60 percent of pilots are uncomfortable flying planes. This hindrance can be disastrous. This specific metric has many different aspects. Most of what causes people to be uncomfortable discussing money started in, you guessed it, childhood!

What do I mean by "uncomfortable discussing money"? It pertains to a salesperson's comfort level in discussing other people's money.

Most of us were taught that money is bad and we shouldn't bring it up—ever. It was taboo to discuss money, and many of us didn't even talk about it with our parents! I had more discussions with my parents about the birds and the bees than I did about money, and we barely talked about the birds and the bees! As we all know, it can be strange and awkward when you need to discuss finances with your loved ones.

When I started with Aflac, I had to practice with my parents and do some fact-finding to see whether they qualified for life insurance. My parents are the Costanzas from *Seinfeld*. I had to ask my mom about her height, weight, health history, and (uh-oh) salary.

When I got to that part of the form, I asked my mom, "Hey Ma, what's your salary?"

My mother responded with a two-word answer, and the second of the two words was "you." I think you can figure out the first word (it wasn't love).

The closest people in your life won't tell you how much money they have in the bank or how much money they make. Why would a salesperson expect a complete stranger, a.k.a. a prospect, to tell them how much money they have to spend on their product or service?

There's a question salespeople ask their prospects that is so intergalactically idiotic that I can't comprehend ever asking it. But salespeople today not only ask their prospects this question, they're taught by some sales training companies to ask it! Ready? You may know what it is. Three words:

"What's your budget?"

There is nothing, I repeat, *nothing* more idiotic than asking this question to a prospect. I can already hear you yelling through the pages, "You don't know my industry! We have to ask it because blah, blah, blah!" But in 99 percent of selling situations, you simply cannot ask a prospect how much money they're willing to give you for the value you haven't yet shown them. It makes no sense. Now that I'm thinking about it, there is one question that's dumber than "What's your budget?" And this one is cringeworthy.

A salesperson looks slightly downward while looking at their prospect and says, "So, Angela, are you expecting?"

Only that question is dumber than "What's your budget?"

Whether You Think You Can or Think You Can't, You're Right

Do you see yourself becoming a top five or ten percenter in sales? Do you see yourself providing immense value to your clients? Do you believe you can achieve your full potential? Do you believe you can earn millions of dollars? Do you believe you can provide a great life for your family?

Remember this: What you believe to be true is true, even if it's not really true. We learned this from the great Henry Ford, who is thought to have said, "Whether you believe you can do a thing or not, you're right." If you believe $1,000 is a lot of money, it's true, even though it's really not true. It's just true in your mind. If you don't think you'll ever make six figures, or multiple six figures, or even seven figures, you won't. If you dedicate yourself to becoming more comfortable with all aspects of money, your results are going to improve dramatically.

This is another aspect of being comfortable discussing money. It comprises what you believe about yourself and your value to the marketplace. I learned this from a mentor, who said to me, "You'll only ever earn within 10 percent, plus or minus, of what you believe you're worth." It's so true. The reason most people don't become millionaires isn't because they aren't smart, don't work hard, or don't have the skills. They don't become millionaires because they don't think they deserve it. If you ask any successful person who's become a millionaire, they'll all tell you the same thing. The first million dollars was the hardest to earn. The second million was easy—the first seemed impossible.

You may or may not feel completely comfortable talking about money just yet, and that's okay; that's normal. You must remember that if you're a sales professional or a leader of sales professionals, this isn't a game. This isn't something you should take for granted if you want to reach your full potential in sales or sales leadership and become a top five percenter. If you're not able to articulate and justify the value of what you're selling, then you could be failing to identify your prospects' compelling reasons to buy from you and failing to understand their ability to pay for your service or product. Your potential to build a long and successful career in sales will be significantly diminished.

You need to get comfortable having those difficult financial conversations. This is all related to how comfortable you are with money. If you don't address this now, it will cost you dearly in the long run. Elite salespeople are comfortable discussing money and having deep financial discussions with their prospects, and they don't get emotional about it. This factor and this factor alone can explain why salespeople all over the world still struggle to reach their full potential. No magic selling system from the 1960s, no one-size-fits-all sales methodology, no fool-proof script, or fake guru's magic objection-handling book will ever fix this issue. You have to get comfortable discussing all aspects of money and having difficult financial conversations with your clients, or you simply won't ever reach the level of sales you want to reach.

These two competencies are only two of the twenty-one that are measured by The Sales DNA Test. But here's the biggest problem of all: What happens if these hindrances are never discovered? When would they get fixed? Never. Can you even comprehend the amount of lifetime income a salesperson would lose if they never overcame their need to be liked? Or how many millions in sales are lost because a salesperson is uncomfortable discussing money? That is why taking The Sales DNA Test is the single most crucial thing any salesperson can do if they want to improve and reach their full potential in sales.

TRUST THE PROCESS
(WHAT WOULD BOB ROSS DO?)

THE PHRASE "WHAT WOULD JESUS DO?" (a.k.a. WWJD) is a
mantra many of us are familiar with. It rose to popularity in the early
part of the twentieth century based on the book by Charles Sheldon
with that phrase as the title. About a hundred years later, in the late
1990s, WWJD was everywhere! It was on bumper stickers, T-shirts,
bracelets, basically anything you could print it on. The idea behind
WWJD is that people should ask themselves that question when faced
with a situation and then model the behavior that Jesus would display.
I certainly understand the thought process, and it seems like this would
be a good principle to follow, regardless of your religious preferences.

I choose to follow a different mantra based on the perceived behavior
of what a particular person would do. And much like Jesus, the person
whose behavior I choose to model was kind, loved all beings, and had a
dedicated following of disciples. The phrase I use is WWBRD: What
would Bob Ross do? I can sense you smiling brightly right now! He
may be my favorite human being ever to walk the planet. Every day,

both in my life and in my business, when faced with a tough situation or a difficult decision, I ask myself: What would Bob Ross do?

You may be laughing, or you may agree with me, but the reason I do this is quite clear. If you don't know who Bob Ross is, go look him up! Known for his trademark hairstyle (which he hated, by the way), Bob Ross was one of the most genuine, charismatic, soothing, welcoming, and calming souls ever to live. He discovered oil painting while he was enlisted in the US Air Force in the early 1960s. In 1975, while still in the military, he saw the TV show *The Magic of Oil Painting*. The show was hosted by a German painter named Bill Alexander, who painted with a technique called alla prima, also known as the "wet-on-wet" technique. Paintings could be completed in less than an hour using that technique. Bob Ross learned the technique, and soon after, he started making more money from his paintings than from his military position. He retired from the Air Force in 1981 with the rank of Master Sergeant.

Bob started teaching some of his friends how to paint, and one friend, Annette Kowalski, became his future business partner. She and her husband ended up pooling their savings with Bob to create Bob Ross, Inc. Ross then launched the PBS television series *The Joy of Painting*, where he taught millions of people how to paint beautiful paintings full of happy accidents. ☺ Ross was beloved for his light humor, gentle demeanor, and soothing voice.

Even after his untimely death from lymphoma in 1995, Bob Ross has remained a household name. He's more popular today than when he was alive, thanks to platforms like YouTube. And if social media had been around when Bob Ross was in his heyday, he would have been one of the first true influencers. This gentleman would have been the first person to have one hundred million followers. We're talking about a man who somehow got millions of people to sit in their houses and watch him paint on TV. Just let that sink in!

I've presented to thousands of people over the years, and I've asked them all one question. (And it's still incredible when I get to take people through this explanation.) Bob Ross is credited with teaching more than ten million people how to paint. What Bob accomplished during his all too short fifty-three years with us was nothing short of miraculous. Even crazier is the fact that almost everyone he taught how to paint had no interest in painting before they discovered Bob!

Did all ten million people who learned how to paint from Bob Ross have God-given artistic ability? No! Of course not. So, if they had no clue how to paint, how could he teach millions of people how to create beautiful landscapes? The answer: He taught them a system. Sales leaders (and all leaders for that matter), please pay attention here. Let's say you have a salesperson (much like one of Bob's students) who has no talent, no skills, and no ability. Let's say you teach them a system to follow, you work with them closely, you support them, you allow them to make mistakes (Happy Accidents), and most importantly, you make it enjoyable. What do you think happens to their performance?

Now, let's take another type of salesperson. They have talent, skills, and ability, and you teach them a system to follow to maximize their capabilities and get the most out of their skill sets. What do you think happens to their performance? These are your top performers. Imagine that! Teaching people a sales process while making it enjoyable helps them sell more—no matter where they are currently.

The single best thing about my borderline obsession with Bob Ross is seeing how many lives he impacted in a positive way. After watching one of the Bob Ross documentaries, I decided to read all the comments people posted online. I swear to you, I spent forty-five minutes reading hundreds of comments from people about Bob and how much he impacted their lives. One comment stuck out for me, and I never forgot it—it struck me like a bolt of lightning. Other people noticed the comment, too, and it was featured in an article in *The Atlantic*.

The commenter wrote, "'If art teachers were all like Ross, no one would fail, no one would feel ashamed to show their work, no one would dread coming to art class.'" *The Atlantic* quoted another commenter as saying, "'He didn't paint to show how good of a painter he was. He painted to show how good of a painter you could be.'"[1] Wow.

If you have kids or grandkids in school right now, how would you feel if you knew this is how their teachers taught them? More importantly, how would your kids or grandkids feel about going to school every day if they were taught like this? Is this how we're taught business? Hell no. Is this how salespeople are taught how to sell? Hell no. Bob's show was called *The Joy of Painting*. It wasn't called *The Anxiety of Painting*, *The Fear of Painting*, or *The Stress of Painting*. Salespeople who are anxious, fearful, or stressed don't sell more. If you teach them that sales can be fun, joyful, and rewarding, guess what happens? You need to create a culture where your sales team feels psychologically safe. If they have a problem, they should feel safe coming to you. Not worried you're going to yell at them for not "fixing it" themselves. They need to feel that it's safe to fail. It's safe to be themselves. It's safe to make a mistake. You must celebrate the small wins and laugh off the losses. Make sales fun, and your team will run through brick walls for you. And they'll have a blast doing it! That's the art of sales leadership.

The Foundation of Sales Success— The Sales Process

If we think of sales management as directing a sales team to achieve targets and goals, the sales process would be the road map to achieving those targets and goals. How do you know whether your team is making progress or what to focus on next? How do you coach people through the process? What are the steps to take in each deal? What are the criteria for each step? Does your team know which stage they're at in each deal? The sales process is an essential component of sales leadership, and it refers to the sequence of steps taken to close a deal. And frankly, it goes way beyond that—critical stages of the sales process happen after the deal is made: delivery, deployment, nurturing, account management, case studies, referrals, and more. The sales process starts the second someone picks up a phone, sends an email, or receives a lead, and it continues through years of nurturing and client relationship maintenance.

Here's an example showing the classic stages of a very basic sales process.

Sample Sales Process

Make sure this is the right customer for you. Is there urgency and ability to buy?

Determine the technical capabilities needed to solve their problems using your differentiated solutions.

Negotiate back and forth over timeline, investment, or any objections they might have. Then, ask for the business.

QUALIFY   SCOPE   WIN   SERVICE

NEW LEAD   DISCOVER   PRESENT   IMPLEMENT

Find out what their unique needs and problems are that need to be solved, and what they've tried before.

Provide an overview of what you heard, their problem and pains, and your solution along with your terms.

Engage with your implementation team to begin delivering and onboarding the solutions you have sold.

This may not be your team's exact sales process, and your process may have specific customizations—this is just an example. You may have a highly complex sales process with ten, fifteen, or twenty stages. A sales process starts when a lead comes in or when a prospect is contacted. The next step is the qualification stage, where you'll make sure the prospect fits your ICP and determine whether they're the right type of prospect. Is there an urgency? Is there a need? Is there an intent to buy? Once you qualify the lead, then you'll typically go into the discovery stage to better understand their need, find out what kind of pain they're suffering from, understand the unique problems they're facing and when or how they need to be solved, and learn about what they may have tried before to solve them.

And, of course, depending on your business, company, or solution, this could be one, two, or three calls. It could be an exploratory call to gather more information, a first call with a champion, or the first discovery call with your decision-maker. It's so important for you to understand your unique sales process from start to finish so critical steps aren't missed by you or your sales team. Typically, after qualification and discovery, enter the scoping stage. This is where you determine the technical capabilities needed to solve the prospect's problem using your differentiated solutions.

After that, you'll go into the presenting stage to share your product or solution. This is where you'll provide an overview of what you've heard from the discovery stage and the scoping stage. You'll share that you understand their problems and pains, and you mirror them back to the prospect, along with your solution. If you're in tech or SaaS sales, this is the demo stage. Afterward, you may have something like a win stage or a negotiation stage. This is where you're going back and forth over the timeline, particulars, pricing, or contract length; you're usually overcoming objections, and then you're asking for the business.

Following that comes the implementation stage, where you launch the solution and deliver your services or product. Last, you're in the servicing stage, customer service stage, account management stage, or nurture stage. That's a basic sales process, and I know yours may be different. The point is to have a process, know it like the back of your hand, and ensure your team executes each stage. If they do, the chances of making a sale increase dramatically.

Sales managers, pay attention! The following is what you can expect if you finally take the time to get a sales process built once and for all.

First, your ramp-up time for new salespeople will be much faster. No more throwing your salespeople to the wolves. Imagine creating autonomy and self-confidence among your new salespeople from week one!

Next, you'll have a recipe for success. It is immensely important for brand-new sales hires to know what needs to be done to have the best chance to succeed. They must also know what's expected of them—if you don't put them in a position to do just that, what exactly are you relying on to help them achieve greatness?

Your salespeople will work with more qualified leads. Just think about the amount of time your salespeople waste on unqualified prospects, deals that have no chance of closing, and problem customers you wish you never had. That's what happens when you let salespeople wing it. With a clearly defined sales process, your salespeople will focus on the clients you *want*.

Your sales team will have higher win rates. Isn't this what you want? Telling your salespeople to do a better job of closing and converting more prospects into clients when you've provided them with next to nothing for a sales process is almost comical.

Following a sales process will lead to better customer experiences, which leads to more referrals from clients with better customer experiences, which leads to increased revenue.

Just as importantly, you'll have happier salespeople and sales leaders. I know this isn't talked about much, but the happiness of your sales team and everyone's daily mindset play a huge role in the success of your organization. If your salespeople are selling more stuff, if they're generating more referrals, if they're getting more customers, and if they're making more money, don't you think they'll be happier? If you spend the time, money, and effort to build a duplicatable, effective sales process, your sales team will reach a success you never thought possible.

If You Build It, Sales Will Come

I'm sure you've heard a slightly different version of this quote before; it comes from the 1989 movie *Field of Dreams*, and the line is usually remembered as, "If you build it, they will come." The movie was based on a book by W. P. Kinsella called *Shoeless Joe*. But that is not the exact phrase used in the movie. Ray Kinsella, played by Kevin Costner, hears a voice as he's walking through his cornfield, telling him, "If you build it, *he* will come."[2] *He* ends up being Shoeless Joe Jackson (a famous baseball player). But in the end, another *he* that shows up is Ray's father. After years of estrangement, he shows up to reconcile with his son. This line is almost always misquoted when referring to building something or taking on something new in your life or business.

The lesson to be learned here, and it will make more sense if you've seen the movie, is that they will not come right away, especially if you're building it for the wrong reasons. In a business sense, if you're building a sales process for the sole reason of increasing your EBITDA, you're building it for the wrong reasons.

The craziest part of the story is that when Ray finally builds his field of dreams, *they all come*. In the last scene of the movie, you see an aerial shot of thousands of cars surrounding his cornfields as far as the eye can see; thousands of people have come to visit his magical place. And the coolest part is that he didn't have a goal of attracting thousands of people, selling tons of tickets, and making lots of money. It didn't matter to him that all these people were coming. Remember, wanting something too much usually gets you the opposite. Not thinking about the outcome usually gets you a greater outcome. Imagine building something that attracts the greatest talent in your vertical, five-star reviews, more referrals than you can imagine, industry accolades, higher retention, superb Net Promoter Scores, supremely engaged salespeople, increased win rates, shorter sales cycles, higher margins, more opportunities converted, and more consistent revenue, just to name a few benefits. So, when it comes to building a sales process, or what may be called your company's *field of dreams*, imagine what will happen when *they all come*.

If you don't have a sales process, your team will have no structure to follow and no consistency. You won't know where deals are or what stages they're in. Your forecasts will be off, deals will take longer to close, and your team will struggle to hit revenue goals. But other than that, there's no need to have one. (Eye roll.)

Before you consider building a sales process or having an expert help you do it (I know a guy ☺), you've got to spend the time it takes to define your target audience/ICP and map out the entire sales process from beginning to end. Then, you must document and track the entry and exit criteria for each stage of the process to know what your sales velocity is and how quickly you're moving through deals. Are your deals moving fast enough? Are they moving too fast? Too slow? And if so, why are they moving slower than usual? You'll want to look at specific metrics like revenue, sales growth, sales cycle length, conversion rates, customer acquisition costs, average deal size, average contract length, or whatever metrics make sense for your business. The most critical part is training your sales team on how to execute *your specific* sales process. This is why generic, one-size-fits-all magic selling systems and methods don't work. You've got to teach, practice, drill, rehearse, role-play, and repeat—but only if you want your sales team to sell lots of stuff.

The NFL has thirty-two teams. Do all thirty-two teams have a playbook? Of course. Do they all have the exact same playbook? Of course not. There isn't one magic way of playing football or some antiquated football methodology from the '60s that every football player robotically executes. More importantly, do you think it would be effective for the quarterback to just tell the other ten players on the field, "Hey guys, just get open or something," or "Go long"?

How many times do you think players practice executing the same play? Once? Twice? NFL athletes put in about sixty hours of practice every week in preparation for their games on Sunday. And guess what? There are only eighteen minutes of live action during a football game—sixty hours of preparation for eighteen minutes of work. That's just one reason NFL athletes make millions of dollars a year, and most salespeople don't.

Unfortunately, that's the opposite of what most companies and most salespeople are doing right now. There is no playbook, they don't practice, most don't role-play or document anything, they don't know where to go or what to do, and very few ever watch game film … and still, they're expected to score lots of touchdowns and win the Super Bowl!

The value of creating a documented sales process and sales playbook is huge:

- You'll have a tool that will provide your salespeople with a step-by-step process to ensure they deliver a powerful sales presentation every time.

- You'll have fully written templates for your sales team that cover every need they might have, from phone calls to emails, Zoom meetings, networking events, proposals, and referrals.

- You'll have an environment that leads to overperformance, and you no longer wonder why your team is underperforming.

- You'll be able to effectively and accurately predict pipelines and deal flow.

- Your sales managers will have something to teach, train, and coach, rather than just using carrots and sticks and accusing their sales team when they don't hit their numbers.

- You'll have a much better chance to get your C players to become B players and your B players to become A players.

- You'll cut your ramp-up time for new salespeople in half, and they'll become more productive and more effective much more quickly than before.

The last step in building your sales process is to improve, adjust, and tweak continuously. You should be constantly on the lookout for opportunities to enhance, modify, and pivot, if necessary, based on market conditions. Is the market softening? Is your industry different from what it was six months ago? Are your customers buying differently? Is the supply chain affecting your production or delivery? Are your customers facing new challenges?

Being aware of all these factors allows you to make the necessary adjustments needed to put your salespeople in the best position to win. Frankly, most companies have their heads in the sand and don't change until it's too late. Doing what you've always done will get you where you already are, and if you don't adapt, well, you can look up what Charles Darwin said about the survival of the fittest. You must constantly evaluate and update your sales process to be a relevant player in your marketplace, understand your clients' needs, be at the forefront of your industry's trends, and be the outlier in a sea of mediocrity.

9

SALES TRAINING IN TODAY'S MARKETPLACE

IMAGINE IF EVERY MOVIE THEATER in every city played the same movie all day, every day. You don't get to choose the movie either—you just buy your ticket and get to watch *Gigli*. Sounds amazing, doesn't it? Or how about a show on Netflix or Hulu that streams constantly, 24/7? No choices, no seasons, just one episode, over and over again. I'm sure people would love that.

By this point, you probably understand why magic selling systems and one-size-fits-all sales methodologies simply don't make sense. You cannot be all things to all people in every aspect of their existence, yet some sales training companies tout their special way of selling as if it were the only way it should be done.

I started The Sales Collective because I was tired of seeing organizations hire sales training company after sales training company and still not get the results they were looking for. Many companies pretend to have a magic selling system that works for all salespeople in all sales roles in all organizations, but that isn't what happens. Moreover, how could sales trainers ever pretend to know how to teach, train, inspire, and motivate your sales team when they have no idea what's going on inside your specific organization?

Before you attempt to hire any sales training company, you need to know the answers to the following questions:

- Are your salespeople following a stage-driven, documented sales process?

- Are your salespeople in the roles that make the best use of their skills?

- Are your salespeople self-motivated, driven, autonomous, and self-sufficient?

- Are your salespeople delivering a consistent value proposition and brand message and not saying completely different things?

- Are your salespeople able to deliver presentations with a high degree of skill, confidence, and competence without giving away all your margins?

- Are your sales leaders highly effective in motivating, inspiring, coaching, and driving your team and not just salespeople forced into leadership roles?

- Are your sales leaders in complete alignment with the executive team in terms of strategy, process, growth, and future goals?

- Are your sales leaders world-class communicators and professionally trained to coach (and not manage) their team?

- Are your sales leaders following a consistent plan for growth by implementing regular role-play exercises, effective pipeline and deal flow reviews, and one-on-one mentorship?

If your company doesn't know the answers to these questions, and more importantly, if the sales training company doesn't know the answers, how would they be able to improve your sales team's results and performance?

This is why our company will always conduct a Sales Team Evaluation before we attempt to determine whether we can help a client. Think of this process as the MRI of a sales team, where we look inside to find out exactly what's causing your pain. If you hurt your knee and you couldn't walk, you'd go to the doctor. And if the doctor never looked at you, never asked any questions, and didn't do an MRI and instead told you to take two aspirins and you'd be fine in a couple of hours, what would you do?! Therein lies the problem with most sales training companies. If a doctor gave two aspirins to every patient who walked into her office without examining what was causing the pain, not only would it be ineffective, but it could also cause more damage than good. But almost all sales training companies will tell you that their magic sales methodology will cure all ailments in all people, and no matter what the problem is, they'll fix it. Ya, okay.

You need to look under the hood before telling people you can fix their engine. The individuals on your sales team have sales skills, but beyond that, they have emotions, tendencies, thought processes, habits, belief systems, and biases that determine their effectiveness in sales. These factors need to be identified, addressed, and corrected if you ultimately want them to reach their full potential. That's why every member of the sales organization takes The Sales DNA Test, which you've already read about.

Imagine that you knew every single factor hindering the performance of every one of your people—the factors that are preventing them from reaching their full potential. If you know what the issues are, you can finally identify their challenges and self-limiting beliefs and start addressing and improving them. For sales training to be effective, you must know *specific* information about the *specific* talents and thought processes of the *specific* salespeople on your *specific* team who sell your *specific* product or service! Without this level of specificity, you're back to relying on the one-size-fits-none philosophy.

What Jim Furyk Taught Me About Sales Training

There is no "right way" to swing in golf, just like there's no "right way" to sell. The fundamental flaw with the one-size-fits-all sales training method is that every human being is different! Every sales situation in the history of human civilization was different. Every salesperson who's ever sold an item, a widget, a solution, a product, a service, or a gadget is different. All salespeople should *not* sell the same way, just like all golfers should *not* swing like Jim Furyk.

Let me explain: The holy grail in golf is to shoot a score of 59 in a round. This means it would take a golfer only 59 strokes to complete eighteen holes, as opposed to the expected 72. Only thirteen players in the history of the PGA Tour have shot a 59. Even more legendary is when someone shoots a 58. Only one player has ever shot a 58. One. Ever. Jim Furyk. Oh, and by the way, he is also the *only* player to shoot a 58 *and* a 59! Jim Furyk isn't known for accomplishing this incomprehensible feat. But he *is* known for one thing: the ugliest swing in the history of golf. And that's being polite.

A world-renowned golf announcer, David Feherty, said Jim Furyk's swing is about as graceful as watching an octopus fall out of a tree. So, if he's the only human in history to shoot a 58 and a 59, his swing must be duplicated by every golfer on Earth, right? His swing must be taught to all golfers by every professional golf instructor, right? Nope. You would never teach his swing to a single player. Why? Because it works for Jim and only Jim. His unique, unorthodox, and awkward golf swing has made him one of the best golfers in history.

The same principle applies to sales, but it's never done this way. The mistake made by sales leaders would be the same as if golf instructors taught every student to swing like Jim. If this logic were correct, every golfer would swing like Jim Furyk. But zero percent of them do. Because *you can't swing like Jim.* One of the unending reasons why top-performing salespeople make unsuccessful sales managers is because they say, "Swing like me" or "Sell like me." Your job as a sales leader is to help your team members swing like themselves, *not* like you.

What may be even more damaging to a new salesperson is a ride-along. That's when a sales manager tells a new salesperson to spend the day with Bob.

"Now, Dez, I want you to ride with Bob today and watch his every move. Note how he holds his coffee, parks his car backward, winks at the receptionist, convinces them to place an order, and finishes every meeting in under thirty minutes. He's the best we have, and I want you to emulate everything he does if you want to be as successful as he is."

I am dead f**king serious. This is what's been done for decades! Let me state this one more time: If you're a sales manager and you get nothing else from this book, please remember this: **You have to teach salespeople to execute *their* swing.**

Competency-Based Sales Training

As we just discussed, one-size-fits-all sales training doesn't work and never will. Intermittent training on building rapport, handling objections, and closing is pointless, valueless, and a waste of money. If you truly want to get the most out of your salespeople, you must coach your salespeople to improve their specific competencies. You cannot coach salespeople to a metric. Let me repeat: You cannot coach salespeople to succeed through metrics. Using lagging indicators as a tool to drive results is backward, antiquated, and ineffective. This is why company leaders are constantly banging their heads against the wall, trying to figure out why their salespeople aren't selling more. You must coach your salespeople to execute their leading indicators (a.k.a. DPIs) if you want them to excel. To excel, they need to be trained in three specific types of competencies: processes, skill sets, and behaviors. The specific definitions of these competencies depend on your organization and are based on the role of the salesperson, the sales cycle, the products, and more. Without taking this first step, examining lagging indicators is pointless. Only after coaching your salespeople in the specific competency areas can you measure the lagging indicators to evaluate the impact of that specific training. Are you seeing improvements? Is the team moving the needle? Are they selling more?

This will only work if you first align competency training with leading indicators. Once you see the impact of lagging indicators, you can take that information and use it to drive the next set of training programs. Where do you need to fill in the gaps? Where did the team fall short?

The sales manager should deliver competency-led coaching and training. Coaching to competencies isn't about doing deal reviews or conducting pipeline evaluations. It's not about dangling carrots, "go get 'em pals," or threatening them with a PIP. To drive real improvement in your salespeople's performance, you must coach them on specific competencies. Competency-led training is a strategic and data-driven approach that will drive the needle more than any command-and-control leadership style ever will.

Sales Training and Your Teeth

There are no shortcuts to success in sales. Whether you're a salesperson or a sales manager, you must put in the time, effort, hard work, and practice if you want to become a top five percenter. It takes zero work to be mediocre. But to be great, you should read more books, listen to more podcasts, hire a coach, take online courses, and invest in your skills and personal growth. I'm sorry to say this, but if you think your company will do this for you, you are sadly mistaken. Did you know the average company spends only $2K per year on sales training for their entire team?! That's per year . . . only $2K . . . for the *entire* team! The average company spends more money on coffee than on training their salespeople. Look it up.

The following information is geared toward sales managers, but salespeople might not be surprised by these numbers.

- 82 percent of B2B decision-makers think salespeople are unprepared.[1]

- 73 percent of salespeople in companies that teach them to follow a process and give them consistent coaching achieve their quotas.[2]

- 70 percent of all salespeople say they have not received any formal training in sales—instead, they describe themselves as "self-taught social selling."[3]

- 69 percent of salespeople say their job is harder than in the past.[4]

- According to several studies, every dollar invested in sales training returns approximately $20 *in incremental revenues*.[5]

Here are the key takeaways from this list (and believe me, I could have shared additional alarming statistics with you). First, you need to personally invest your time and money if you truly want to reach your full potential in professional selling. Your company is probably not going to help you. Most leaders of companies today still live in the Dark Ages of business and believe that training and coaching their salespeople is unnecessary. Instead, they think that berating them in meetings, threatening them with PIPs, and assigning unrealistic quotas somehow inspires them to perform. You, and you alone, must take control of your own training and personal growth. I promise that if you do, you'll be much more effective in sales and sales leadership before you know it.

Do you brush your teeth? I'm sure you do—at least I hope you do—and I'm assuming you know you're supposed to brush for two minutes at least twice a day. That's what we've been taught and what seems to work for billions of people. You're supposed to follow this approach because consistency is more effective than intensity.

Here's an experiment you could try: Stop brushing your teeth for a year. For a full twelve months, don't go near the sink. Throw away all your toothpaste, floss, and your toothbrush. No brushing, no flossing, no mouthwash, and no Listerine.

Go to the dentist a year later, but the day before you go, take the day off work. When you wake up, start brushing. Be relentless! Don't stop. Brush for twenty-four hours straight. Then, after your dentist announces that your mouth is a complete disaster, that you need three cavities filled and a root canal, tell her she's got to be wrong. It can't be so. Your mouth is perfectly fine, according to you. She'll question your sanity and ask why you think your mouth is in good shape. You can tell her, "Dr. Mendoza, my mouth is perfectly fine. I took the day off work yesterday, and I brushed for twenty-four hours straight!"

She'll say, "Excuse me? You did what, why?"

And then you'll say, "Well, I had to make up for the last twelve months of not brushing my teeth!"

As we all know, you can't jam a year's worth (1,460 minutes) of brushing your teeth into one day. You also can't brush your teeth so hard that your toothbrush breaks in half, and your gums start to bleed profusely. Brushing your teeth with intensity doesn't make them cleaner. It's about consistency, every day, with regularity.

Therein lies the problem with most sales training. Unfortunately, for some unknown reason, most companies think that intensely training their salespeople will somehow work better than consistently training their salespeople. Tell me if you've experienced this:

BIG ANNOUNCEMENT! Our annual sales kickoff this year is in Miami! Get ready! We've come up with another yearly theme we pulled out of ChatGPT for this year's meeting: "One Team, One Dream." Are you ready to be creative and awe-inspired?! Here's the agenda for our three-day session!

Day One: Arrivals. Meet at the open bar and get trashed!

Day Two: Show up hungover for the morning session. We'll bore everyone to death with an antiquated PowerPoint and emotionless message, followed by a wasted afternoon featuring an excruciatingly valueless review of our performance last year. We'll then proceed with our mandatory team-building event, breaking boards, walking on fire, and enjoying a scavenger hunt. We'll finally wrap up the day with heavy drinking again!

Day Three: Send everyone the message, "You need to do better!" We'll then foist unrealistic goals that clearly aren't appropriate for any of the teams.

Day Four: Head home. Salespeople and sales managers are expected to go right back to doing things as they've always done them. But don't worry, we won't do anything for the next 362 days to help them!

Wow! That really sounds amazing, doesn't it? I wish I were joking, but this is typical. Conduct the annual rah-rah session, tick a box, and convince yourself you're inspiring your sales team. Very few companies train their sales teams once a quarter. Even fewer train their salespeople once a month. Even fewer train their teams once a week, and almost none train their salespeople every day. And still, they can't seem to figure out why their salespeople aren't performing at the level they expect.

Gamification Is the Key

As we learned earlier, measuring lagging indicators to determine future success is simply not a good idea. Focusing on scoring more runs doesn't win you more games. Focusing on executing more quality at bats, which will lead to more runs, helps you win more games. It's the same in sales. Quality at bats in sales are called DPIs, and if salespeople execute their DPIs consistently and with proficiency, guess what happens? They sell a lot more stuff! But remember, not all DPIs are the same for all salespeople and for all sales roles in all companies. Pay attention, sales managers. It's up to you to determine which four to six DPIs you want your salespeople to execute each day, and it's up to you to ensure they're executing them with proficiency. Salespeople who focus on executing four to six DPIs every day will always generate more sales than the salespeople who don't. The companies and leaders who drive and reward these activities will always generate more revenue than the companies that don't.

It boils down to this: How do you identify the appropriate DPIs for your team, and how do you make sure your team is doing them consistently? One way to successfully drive the execution of DPIs is through gamification. As we discussed in Chapter 1, we are revolutionizing the performance of sales teams around the world with this concept.

Gamification addresses the three major challenges all sales leaders face when trying to maximize the performance of their sales teams: holding their salespeople accountable, convincing their salespeople to adopt and use their CRM and other sales technology, and help-ing their salespeople implement the training and strategies they are taught. We use gamification to reward salespeople for doing more of the high-impact activities we know will drive better results and more revenue. They're rewarded with coins for completing their daily activities, and they get bonus coins when they hit their goals based on those activities.

For example, they might get ten coins for making one hundred prospecting calls, but if they make one hundred prospecting calls ten times in a month, they're rewarded with five hundred bonus coins. They also have access to cool prizes, rewards, and recognition, which makes it more fun and addictive for the entire team—in a good way. Once they've accumulated a certain number of coins, much like you'd accumulate tickets in an arcade or at Dave & Busters, they get to spend those coins in a reward store. Your company and leadership team choose the specific gifts and rewards, and you base them on what your salespeople want instead of a meaningless $25 gift card or movie passes. Yes, some companies still do this.

Hundreds of companies and thousands of salespeople around the world have more fun selling, driving increased daily activity, and seeing results skyrocket in a very short amount of time. If you'd like to learn more about gamification and how it can help drive more engagement and production from your sales team, we'll be happy to help!

Four Steps to Improve Sales Team Training

Sales managers, this is primarily written for you. Developing a high-performing sales team is essential for any business looking to thrive in today's competitive marketplace. But how do you train your salespeople to become more effective? The answer lies in a structured approach that considers the unique needs and challenges of your team. There are four key steps to training your salespeople more effectively and equipping them with the skills and knowledge they need to succeed.

Step One: Assess Your Sales Team's Needs

The first step in training your salespeople is to assess their needs. This involves identifying the areas where your team needs the most support and development. As you know, there are thousands of assessments you can use. We use The Sales DNA Test because it's the best and only one in the marketplace capable of assessing your salespeople on their ability to sell. As a reminder, The Sales DNA Test does not look at a salesperson's personality traits, behavioral style, or psychological makeup. It does have a component that reveals aptitude, but the emphasis is on whether an individual will *execute the skills they have* and which weaknesses will *prevent execution.* Do they need to be liked? Are they uncomfortable discussing money? Do they sell consultatively? Will they recover from rejection quickly? Do they know how to reach decision-makers? Are they motivated extrinsically, intrinsically, or altruistically?

Just as important as The Sales DNA Test is a version of the assessment called The Sales Manager DNA Test, which evaluates the skill set and effectiveness of the sales manager. Do they coach effectively? Do they hold people accountable consistently? Do they know how to manage a pipeline? Do they provide and accept feedback effectively? Do they run productive and valuable sales meetings and one-on-one sessions?

Company leaders need to know and understand the strengths, skills, weaknesses, hindrances, and self-limiting beliefs of their specific salespeople and sales leaders. Without this information, how would they ever expect their sales team to reach its full potential? They would have no idea what's holding back their sales team and keeping them from achieving greatness.

In addition to using the Sales DNA assessments, you can analyze your sales team's performance data. Conversion rates, sales volume, average order size, sales cycle length, and net-new business are just a few metrics you can use to compare the sales team's actual performance to expected performance. You can also conduct surveys or interviews with your sales team to gather their input on the areas in which they feel they need the most assistance.

Step Two: Develop a Real Sales Training and Coaching Program

Once you've identified the areas in which your sales team needs improvement, you can start to design a training program that is tailored to meet the specific needs of each individual salesperson. Remember that the one-size-fits-all approach simply doesn't work and will never get you the results you're looking for. You must teach them to swing like *them*, not like you. The biggest challenge with developing a *real* sales training and coaching program is the time investment it takes to get it done right. Building a targeted and effective training program specifically for your team and executing that program takes concerted effort, intention, and deep work. And because sales managers are stretched to their limits every day, it's often impossible for them to complete this process without some help. In such cases, without help, the new training approach will fail. You probably already know that one-day or quarterly rah-rah sessions filled with inspirational quotes and motivational stories don't work. This method of training, which is, unfortunately, what most companies do, will simply cause information overload. When this approach is used, limited information is retained, and the training doesn't move the needle one bit.

Your sales training and coaching program could include classroom-style training sessions, online courses, or virtual workshops. Here are some of the key elements to consider when designing your training program:

- **Objectives:** Set clear objectives for your sales training and coaching program to ensure they align with your overall business objectives.

- **Training methods:** Choose the training methods that are most effective for your specific team, such as role-playing, case studies, or virtual sessions.

- **Timing and frequency:** Determine the timing and frequency of your training program and ensure it fits within your team's schedule and workload.

- **Measurement and evaluation:** Establish the proper metrics (including DPIs) to measure the success of your training program and regularly evaluate its effectiveness to make improvements as needed.

Step Three: Deliver the Training Program

When delivering a training program, a few key obstacles can derail it quickly. The first challenge concerns content creation. It takes a long time to build every single deck, talk track, role-play session, and learning exercise. The next obstacle relates to the delivery of sales training. It should be delivered with consistency, not intensity, as you've now learned. It should be disseminated using something called microlearning, which involves shorter lessons and shorter training periods. Sitting in a training session for three consecutive hours is ineffective, and retention is minimal. The next potential challenge is the clear communication of objectives and expectations of the training program prior to the training so the entire team is in alignment with expectations. Another potential hardship is providing your team with the necessary resources and support if you want them to participate fully. There should be a course catalog or agenda, and you should establish a schedule and timeline for training. You must reinforce what they're learning and ensure they are implementing the lessons in the field every week. The last obstacle many sales managers face is holding their teams accountable. You can't just assume they're learning, assume they're retaining, and assume they're implementing what you've taught them. You have to train them well, provide role-playing opportunities to observe their adoption and proficiency, and use positive reinforcement when you see them using what they've learned.

When delivering your training, it's also crucial to keep your sales team engaged and motivated. Consider using a variety of training techniques to keep your team involved, such as interactive activities, group discussions, open forums, and hands-on role-play sessions. It's also critical to provide ongoing support and feedback (and for you to receive feedback) throughout the training process. This can include regular coaching sessions, progress reviews, and opportunities for your sales team to provide feedback on what they're enjoying or what they may not be enjoying about the training program. You'll want to create videos and supporting documents for your team to review after sections of training are completed. Without seeing something multiple times in multiple different ways, it's hard for some people to retain the knowledge they need to be able to implement the new process in the field with consistency.

The last key to delivering an effective sales training and coaching program is to get 100 percent buy-in from the entire team. Leadership, sales managers, and salespeople all need to be on the same page if you want full adoption and great engagement. Everyone needs to be involved in the process of both creating and receiving training. The sales manager needs to fully understand how to effectively teach, coach, train, and hold their team accountable for this to work. Unfortunately, most sales managers aren't effective in most of these roles because they've never been professionally coached as a sales leader; most of them were salespeople who were promoted into sales management. When sales managers are effective trainers (not just effective sellers) and know exactly how to ensure the correct behaviors are monitored and encouraged, results will come quickly.

Step Four: Measure the Results

The final step in building an effective, lasting, and comprehensive sales training program is to measure the results. Now, don't get all upset here because I said KPIs are dumb and results don't matter. They matter, but they can't be the only things that matter, and their context is crucial! If you're executing DPIs as well as you can, and results still aren't coming, clearly there's a problem. But that's the role of a sales manager, and monitoring your salespeople's quality at bats is a critical part of your role. To measure the results of a sales training and coaching program, you need to know what results you are trying to measure.

Are you trying to increase top-line revenue? Are you trying to increase the average order size? Are you trying to increase conversions? Are you trying to increase the length of engagements? You can measure a million different things to see whether your program is working, but my point is this: Focus on the metrics you identified as needing improvement—the specific metrics you built your training program to address. The importance of the metrics is why, once again, generic, one-size-fits-all, *go-get-'em-pal* training programs won't do a thing. Ensure you're also conducting post-training evaluations and gathering feedback from the entire team on the effectiveness of the training program. What did they love? What did they hate? What would they have liked to see? Based on the results and feedback, you can adjust your training program to ensure it continues to evolve to meet the specific needs of your sales team and your business.

Implementing an effective sales training and coaching program is a requirement if you truly want to build a high-performing sales team. Untrained and ineffective salespeople won't lead to double-digit growth, increased profitability, and scalability. And ineffective sales managers who aren't equipped to deliver this training won't be the catalyst for record-breaking revenue generation. By assessing your sales team's needs, developing a real sales training and coaching program, delivering the training effectively, and measuring the results, you can almost guarantee your sales team will have more success, and you'll maximize their ability and potential. Staying committed to developing your sales team and providing them with the resources and support they need to thrive will lead to growth in your business beyond your wildest dreams.

SALES LEADERSHIP VS. SALES MANAGEMENT

ACCORDING TO A RECENT STUDY conducted by the Chartered Management Institute in the UK, nearly all people in a leadership position are in that position "accidentally," meaning most of the people currently in managerial or supervisory positions have received no training. Let that sink in! According to their research, a whopping 82 percent of people in leadership roles are accidental managers—and a quarter of those people are in senior leadership roles.[1]

I'm sure you're not surprised by this. I know you've never seen someone promoted to a managerial position because they were good in a non-managerial role, right? This thought hit me one day on the plane: They don't promote the flight attendant to become the pilot. Why would an airline ever consider that? On what basis would this ever make sense? Would they do it because they're a model employee? Would they do it because they've worked at the airline for ten years? Would they do it because the flight attendant really wants to be the pilot? Would they do it because they've worked on the plane, and they *sort of* know how it flies? Would they do it because the promotion comes with a salary increase? Would they do it because they're afraid the flight attendant will leave and go to another airline?

A decision to promote a flight attendant to the pilot role would defy any semblance of logic and common sense, yet this is what companies do on their sales teams repeatedly, and they can't seem to figure out why it doesn't work! Promoting a salesperson to a sales manager position is like promoting the maître d' to executive chef because they're great at their job, the customers like them, they've worked in the restaurant for ten years, really like to cook, and believe they can be a great executive chef. Zero restaurant owners would ever do this if they wanted their restaurant to succeed and stay in business. So, why do companies continue to do this *to* (not *for*) their salespeople?!

One reason (although it's a terrible reason) is that the leadership team thinks that because the potential new sales manager excelled in their previous role as a salesperson, they must be great at managing other salespeople. Um, no. A second reason might be because they already have a login to the CRM and are already on the employee roster, so why bother bringing someone new into the company (someone proven to be an amazing leader of people) when they have someone right there, and they don't need to create another email handle? Or maybe it's because they believe that the salesperson's prior success in a completely different role will lead to success in the sales manager role. I guess that's why Michael Jordan became a Hall of Fame coach, right? Oh wait, he didn't.

It's worth mentioning one last reason why company leaders sometimes promote a top salesperson to a sales manager position—they think the salesperson will feel honored and appreciated and will see a path for their career growth, right? *Please.* It's not a promotion; it's more like a prison sentence. That's why a large percentage of salespeople who were promoted to sales manager not only fail miserably but also beg their leadership team to put them back into sales.

The impact of these accidental leaders can be devastating not only to company culture but also to the bottom line. When organizations are overloaded with poor leaders, especially in sales, it leads to decreased morale, poor performance, and increased turnover. According to research by the Chartered Management Institute, employees who described their manager as ineffective scored significantly lower than those with effective managers in several key measures: job satisfaction (27 percent vs. 74 percent), feeling valued (15 percent vs. 72 percent), and motivation (34 percent vs. 77 percent). Even more alarming is that half the employees surveyed who said their manager was ineffective were planning to hand in their resignations in the next year! In comparison, less than a quarter of those who rated their managers as effective planned to resign. What's more, one in three of the employees surveyed had already left a job because of bad management. The same research showed that a fifth of managers aren't confident in their leadership abilities and that many struggle when dealing sensitively with the multiple issues facing their team members at work and in their home lives. As a result, a third of managers are looking to leave their jobs in the next year.[2]

If you're a CEO or business owner, pay attention! If you promote or hire untrained and unqualified salespeople to sales management positions, here's what will happen:

- You cannibalize your team (by losing a great salesperson and promoting a poor sales manager).

- You alienate the rest of your salespeople because one of their peers is now their boss.

- You promote someone as a feather-in-the-cap reward when, in fact, you've taken them out of their element and thrown them to the wolves.

- You place a huge responsibility on someone who thrives on holding only themselves accountable, but now they need to hold others accountable. (This doesn't work.)

- You expect them to excel in a role utterly different from what they were doing—a role that requires a different mindset, skill set, and belief system.

- You assume that because they can sell, they can teach. (This is not true.)

- You place them in a coaching role when they've had zero formal training on how to coach.

A great maître d' doesn't automatically make a great executive chef. A great cello player doesn't automatically make a great conductor. A great lead actor doesn't automatically make a great director. And great salespeople don't automatically make great sales managers. Got it?

Learn to Lead

Leadership is a learned skill. Many of us work hard to develop our leadership skills because they're so valuable to us as business owners, parents, coaches, etc. Many have participated in classes, workshops,

Vistage groups, training, and coaching, and yet we still don't have an inkling of how great of a leader we can become. That's because it's impossible to become a perfect leader. No matter how hard you try, you will never reach the zenith of perfect leadership.

As leaders, we assume we know what we're supposed to do. I'd like to share some things we all most likely agree we shouldn't be doing. Sales managers make three common mistakes. Most of the time, they don't realize how damaging those mistakes can be. You may already be an amazing sales manager, but it's so important to always reflect on your performance. It's your job to do everything in your power to become the leader your team needs and to do whatever it takes to help them succeed as individuals.

The first big mistake many sales managers make is *fixing* their salespeople's problems instead of *coaching* them. As the old proverb goes, "If you give a man a fish, he eats for a day. If you teach a man to fish, he eats for a lifetime." Don't feed your salespeople. Don't give them every answer on a silver platter, and don't fix the problem they approach you with. Invest the time to help them identify the incorrect behavior or action and coach them on how to implement the necessary change so it doesn't happen again.

The second major mistake many sales managers make is they're disorganized and distracted; they lack a system for themselves as leaders. If you live in a home that's a complete mess, your bedroom is likely a mess. If your bedroom is a mess, your car is likely a mess. And if your car is a mess and your bedroom is a mess, your life is likely a mess. And guess what? Your business is likely also a mess. You can't get mad at your salespeople for being disorganized and distracted when you're disorganized and distracted. Hypocritical leadership isn't leadership.

The last big mistake, and maybe the biggest mistake many sales managers make, is managing by the philosophy, "Do as I say, not as I do." Way too many sales leaders take this approach, and it's hurting their teams much more than they think. They manage by proxy, they manage from afar, and they manage by fear. I've seen it a million times. Some sales managers couldn't close a deal to save their lives, but they admonish their sales teams for not closing deals effectively. They couldn't make an effective cold call if you paid them a million bucks, yet they berate their team for not making effective cold calls. They haven't generated a referral in ten years, but they get upset with their salespeople when they don't.

If you truly want to be an effective and inspiring sales manager, you need to get in the trenches with your team. Make calls, go into the field with them, and show them you can do what they do. Stop managing by "Do as I say, not as I do." Lead with "Do as I *do*, not as I say." If you want your salespeople to produce, then *show them* how to produce. If you want them to run effective discovery meetings, then *show them* how to run effective discovery meetings. If you want to hold them accountable, you need to hold yourself accountable. It's that simple.

The most successful sales managers in the world spend 80 percent of their time on four main activities—accountability, coaching, motivating, and recruiting. Thirty percent of sales managers spend less than 10 percent of their time holding their salespeople accountable, 25 percent of sales managers spend less than 25 percent of their time coaching their salespeople, 30 percent of sales managers spend less than 10 percent on motivational activities, and 50 percent of sales managers spend less than 5 percent of their time on recruiting top talent.[3] If you can master these specific responsibilities and avoid the mistakes most sales managers make, you'll ensure that your team maximizes their opportunities for success. Ultimately, you will become a true sales leader, not just another sales manager.

Are You a Manager or a Leader?

I can't think of anybody in human civilization who said, "I love being micromanaged." Unfortunately, that's what a lot of sales managers believe leadership is all about. The word micromanagement makes my skin crawl and incites the regurgitation of what I just ate for lunch. In *Braveheart*, the infamous Sir William Wallace said, "Men don't follow titles. They follow courage."[4] Does your team look at you as a manager, or do they look at you as their leader? There's a gigantic difference. Do you demand of yourself what you expect from your team? Do you continually invest time and money into your personal growth? Do you strive to become the best leader you can possibly be?

George Flynn was a three-star general in the Marine Corps, and he had a great test for leadership. General Flynn's test to determine whether you're a leader is very simple. If you ask somebody how their day is going and you actually care about the answer, you are a leader. If you dedicate the time and energy it takes to become a great leader, you'll lead a team of brothers and sisters instead of employees and colleagues.

In my opinion, there are thirty specific characteristics that are present in the best leaders

- Honesty
- Integrity

- Humility
- Curiosity

- Commitment
- Passion
- Resilience
- Vulnerability
- Empathy
- Caring
- Hardworking
- A great communicator
- Creative
- Accountable
- Accommodating
- Firm but fair
- Inspiring

- Healthy
- Supportive
- Uplifting
- Innovative
- A great decision-maker
- Transparent
- Persistent
- Empowering
- Patient
- Trustworthy
- A visionary
- A great listener
- Motivated

Of these thirty characteristics, which ones do you truly possess, and which ones do you need to work on? If we asked your team to describe you, would they use any of these words?

There's a lot more to sales leadership than just having the title or your name stenciled on the door of some corner office. Sales leadership is an honor. We should be humbled by the position bestowed upon us. It's a position of great opportunity and great responsibility. It's the gas that powers the sales engine. Without gas, the engine doesn't work. (Don't give me a hard time about electric vehicles—it's just a metaphor.) It works the same with your sales team. You hold the key to unlocking your team's full potential, and you must realize that. Too many sales teams are running on fumes, and they're begging for a fill-up or a recharge. Leadership ability is not something you're born with, and it's not something you can learn overnight. The sales leader is the most important role on a sales team. Even if you have a group of amazingly talented individual salespeople, they'll never reach their full potential if their leadership is lacking.

I'm sure you've heard of the Iditarod. If you haven't, it's known as the last great race, and takes place every March. It's a thousand-mile race from one side of Alaska to the other, and each team consists of fourteen sled dogs and one musher. The relationship between the dog musher and their dogs goes well beyond owner and pet. They are one team, one unit, all for one, and one for all. The mushers do absolutely everything for their dogs, and their dogs do absolutely everything for their mushers. They're clearly willing to die for one another, and they'll do whatever it takes to complete that race. Do you have any idea what would happen if the dogs were allowed to just run the race alone, without a musher, without a leader to guide them? Complete chaos would ensue. That's why it's critical to learn the necessary components of being a leader. Your team needs to know that you're willing to die for them. Figuratively, at least.

Any musher and dog team needs several crucial traits to be effective:

- Mutual respect
- Mutual trust
- Credibility
- Track record of success

- Strategic thinking
- Knowledge transfer
- Recognition
- Empathy

Does your sales team really respect you, and do you respect every person on your sales team? Do you trust your team? If you don't, how can you expect them to trust you? Have you ever lost the trust of someone you've managed? If so, how hard was it to regain their trust? How credible are you? Have you done what you asked them to do? Do you always keep your word? Have you earned your leadership role, or was it accidental? Do you regurgitate actions they should do but have never actually done those actions yourself?

Many sales leaders spend too much time on tactics and not enough time on strategy. Do you lead by example, or are you guilty of the "Do as I *say*, not as I do" leadership style? Do you provide specific direction and guidance? Do you spend enough time in the field with your team? Are you in the foxhole with them? Do you demonstrate knowledge and expertise? Do you give them new ideas, strategies, and tactics so they can improve? Do you take responsibility for your team's failures, or do you place the blame on them? Do you credit them for their success, or do you take all the credit? When they don't perform, do you point the finger at them, or do you point the finger back at yourself? Can you meet them where they're at, emotionally? Can you discover what's bothering them personally? Can you accurately identify what's holding back each member of your sales team?

Or are you the sales manager who thinks the line "Just close more deals" will solve everything?

Those crucial traits are present in every dog musher in the Iditarod. If the musher fails to learn these traits the dogs can see right through them. Have you learned these traits? If not, your team will likely see right through you. Most sales managers feel they're better than they really are at leadership; that's just human nature. We all think we're better than we really are. It takes a lot of guts, courage, vulnerability, and self-awareness to admit you aren't the best leader you could be. Remember, more than 80 percent of leaders have received no formal training! How can you believe you're world-class in an activity that you haven't received any training in?! That's the difference between great sales leaders and mediocre sales managers: Great leaders recognize they have their own challenges and faults (we all do), and then they do everything in their power to improve.

It takes a lot of work and dedication to become a great leader, and you're either willing to put in the time and effort or you're not. People are not born great leaders, just like Serena Williams wasn't born to be the best tennis player of all time. She worked, she trained, she struggled, she bled, she failed, she corrected, she improved, and then she conquered. She put in years of training, blood, sweat, and tears before winning a Grand Slam tournament. You may be close, or you may be far away from where you want to be as a sales leader, but if you commit to putting in the same effort champions put in, you'll get there.

Salespeople Are from Mercury, and Sales Managers Are from Uranus

New salespeople fail for an enormous number of reasons. Sales managers think salespeople don't perform because of x, y, and z, yet salespeople feel they don't perform because of a, b, and c. Sales managers feel one way, and salespeople feel the completely opposite way. The chasm is enormous. The distance between Mercury and Uranus is about 1.7 billion miles, which is why I use this metaphor for salespeople and sales managers.

We asked sales managers what they believe are the top reasons for salespeople not reaching their full potential. Here's what they told us:

- They're lazy.

- They don't work hard.

- They don't listen.

- They don't care.

- They're millennials.

- They aren't skilled enough.

We then asked salespeople why they feel they aren't reaching their full potential. Their perspective, unsurprisingly, is quite different from that of their sales manager. Here's what they told us:

- They have no system to follow.

- They aren't trained properly.

- They receive almost no onboarding.

- They aren't coached.

- They aren't valued.

- They aren't recognized.

Notice the difference between those two lists? They're immensely opposed and completely lack overlap. How is it possible to be on two opposite sides of the spectrum? Why is there such a massive disconnect? What keeps causing this?

Unfortunately, it starts with copycat syndrome. Salespeople will do what their leaders do. Your sales team is a reflection of you, whether you like it or not. If your sales team is not currently performing up to its capabilities, you've got to look at yourself in the mirror. Most likely, they're emulating your bad habits and behaviors. This isn't always true, of course, and it doesn't mean it's always 100 percent the fault of the sales manager. Some salespeople are bad at sales. Some *are* lazy. Some *are* unmotivated. Some *are* unskilled. The failure of the sales team could also be related to a toxic company culture, your nonexistent sales process, or a lack of accountability. Still, it's most certainly your responsibility as a sales manager to ensure you are leading them to the best of your ability.

If we were to ask your sales team to grade you on your leadership ability right now, what grade would they give you? Would it be an A, a C, an F? Would you even *want* to know the answer? If we were to ask them if they feel like you have their back in every single situation, what would they say? What grade would you give yourself right now on your leadership ability and effectiveness? If you can't confidently answer these questions with certainty, or you're not quite the leader you want to become just yet, that's totally okay and quite normal. Very few of us sales leaders are currently at that point, but if you're willing to learn, grow, improve, invest, change, and commit to becoming the best sales leader you can be, it's just a matter of time before you get there.

THE NEW WORLD OF SALES

IT'S YOUR TIME. TO LEAD THE CHARGE. To incite a movement. To break free from the shackles of outdated tactics and archaic mindsets that have been holding you back for far too long. It's time to stand up to toxic sales environments, high-pressure closing tactics, and unrealistic quotas that leave us feeling ashamed and defeated. It's time to fight for transparency and the freedom to foster genuine connections and trust within your team and with your customers, and to embrace a new way of selling and leading that aligns with your values and vision.

The seismic shift in the world of professional selling presents a chance for us salespeople and leaders alike to reinvent ourselves and become the architects of our own success. It's time to shed old-school mentalities and step into the future with an open mind and a willingness to learn. It's time to thrive and create world-class experiences for our clients, foster meaningful symbiotic relationships in our communities, and make a positive difference in the lives of those we serve, both outside and inside our companies.

To be successful in the world of sales today means we must become more than just sellers; we are consultants, educators, and trusted advisors. We harness technology as a tool to augment our abilities rather than using it as a crutch to lean on. We believe kindness is a core value, not a strategy. Sales managers, you are not just bosses; you are mentors, teachers, and supporters. Your investment in personal growth and skill development will drive change and inspire your salespeople to reach their full potential. We live in a world where consumers are more informed, discerning, and savvier than ever. In this new world of sales, those who cling stubbornly to the practices of yesteryear will find themselves on the fringes of relevance, while those who bravely adapt, evolve, and embrace change will thrive.

I've worked with thousands of salespeople and sales managers and found the following qualities and skills are integral to success—empathy, adaptability, transparency, and a deep commitment to understanding and serving the needs of their customers and sales teams.

I invite you to join the ranks of modern sales professionals leading the charge and stepping boldly into the new era of sales with open hearts and brave minds. Together, we can embrace the change, adapt to the shifting landscape, and rewrite the sales narrative for the better. The world may label us as salespeople, but our true mission is to be problem-solvers, relationship builders, and value creators. The future belongs to those who are willing to evolve, innovate, and connect with authenticity. Thank you for embarking on this journey with me.

NOTES

CHAPTER 1: DISPELLING THE MYTHS ABOUT SELLING

1. *Glengarry Glen Ross* (film), Wikipedia article, accessed March 19, 2024, https://en.wikipedia.org/wiki/Glengarry_Glen_Ross_(film).

2. "Always be closing," *Glengarry Glen Ross*, directed by James Foley (1992; Zupnik Enterprises), https://www.youtube.com/watch?v=AO_t7GtXO6w.

3. Dan Diamond, "Just 8% of People Achieve Their New Year's Resolutions. Here's How They Do It," *Forbes*, January 1, 2013, https://www.forbes.com/sites/dandiamond/2013/01/01/just-8-of-people-achieve-their-new-years-resolutions-heres-how-they-did-it/?sh=6efea0bd596b.

4. Nina Joanna, "How Many People Reach Their Goals? Goal Statistics 2023," Goals Calling, May 10, 2022, https://goalscalling.com/goal-statistics/.

5. Marcel Schwantes, "Science Says Only 8 Percent of People Actually Achieve Their Goals. Here Are 7 Things They Do Differently," *Inc.* magazine, June 13, 2018, https://www.inc.com/marcel-schwantes/science-says-only-8-percent-of-people-actually-achieve-their-goals-here-are-7-things-they-do-differently.html.

CHAPTER 2: DETACHING FROM OUTCOMES

1. "Bold Strategy Cotton," *Dodgeball*, directed by Rawson Marshall Thurber (2004; Red Hour Productions), https://www.youtube.com/watch?v=4Ru8DMW-grY.

2. Jim Rohn, "The Set of the Sail," TheHappinessNetwork, May 12, 2012, https://www.youtube.com/watch?v=a-hwzFc8MWk.

3. "'I Learned It by Watching You' Anti-Drug PSA," posted by ticklemeozmo on October 1, 2006, https://www.youtube.com/watch?v=Y-Elr5K2Vuo.

4. Deepak Chopra, *Seven Spiritual Laws of Success* (Artworld, 2019), 59–60.

5. Henry David Thoreau, *Walden* (New York: Thomas W. Crowell and Co., 1910), 8.

CHAPTER 3: BEWARE THE FAKE GURUS

1. Dahvi Shira, "INSIDE STORY: Infomercial King Don Lapre's High-Octane Life— and Shocking Suicide," *People*, October 15, 2011, https://people.com/crime/ don-lapres-high-octane-life-and-shocking-suicide/.

2. Mike Winnet, *Contrepreneur*, YouTube channel, accessed March 19, 2024, https:// www.youtube.com/@MikeWinnet.

CHAPTER 4: SALESPEOPLE AND MUSHROOMS

1. "Office Space (3/5) Movie CLIP—Motivation Problems (1999)," *Office Space*, directed by Mike Judge (1999; Judgmental Films), https://www.youtube.com/ watch?v=cgg9byUy-V4.

2. Kiara Taylor, "Should Sales Teams Expect Higher Churn in 2023?," HubSpot, April 11, 2023, https://blog.hubspot.com/sales/are-people-leaving- sales#:~:text=HubSpot%20research%20confirmed%20this%2035,reaches%20far%20 beyond%20the%20average.

3. "Why 90% of Companies That Use a Guided Sales Process Are Top Performers," HireDNA, November 10, 2022, https://hiredna.com/why-90-of-companies-that-use -a-guided-sales-process-are-top-performers/.

CHAPTER 6: MOTIVATING AND INSPIRING TODAY'S SALESPEOPLE

1. Sam Mallikarjunan, ""The Best Way to Use Money as a Motivator Is to Take the Issue of Money off the Table," *Medium*, May 12, 2016, https://medium.com/@ Mallikarjunan/the-best-way-to-use-money-as-a-motivator-is-to-take-the-issue-of- money-off-the-table-a8ed0ba4b21c.

2. Objective Management Group, https://www.objectivemanagement.com/.

3. Dave Kurlan, "Money Motivated Salespeople a Dying Breed," Kurlan
   & Associates, Inc., April 8, 2011, https://www.kurlanassociates.com/
   understanding-the-sales-force/2011/money-motivated-salespeople-a-dying-breed/.

4. "Show Me the Money," *Jerry Maguire*, directed by Cameron Crowe (1996; TriStar
   Pictures, Gracie Films, and Vinyl Films), https://www.youtube.com/watch?v=
   IpwSXWq1wwU.

CHAPTER 7: THE POWER OF SALES DNA

1. "Psychological Test, Personal Data Sheet—Woodworth," Smithsonian Natural
   Museum of American History, accessed March 19, 2024, https://www.si.edu/es/
   object/nmah_692401.

2. Matthew Harris, Caroline Brett, Wendy Johnson, and Ian Deary, "Personality Stability
   from Age 14 to Age 77 Years," *Psychology and Aging*, Vol. 31, no. 8 (2016): 862–74.
   https://doi.org/10.1037/pag0000133.

3. Stephen Bruce, "Hiring the Wrong Salesperson Is a $2-Million Mistake," *HR Daily
   Advisor*, December 9, 2014, https://hrdailyadvisor.blr.com/2014/12/03/hiring-the
   -wrong-salesperson-is-a-2-million-mistake/.

4. Dave Kurlan, "New Data Shows How Relationships and the Need to Be Liked Impact
   Sales Performance," Kurlan & Associates, Inc., June 4, 2018, https://www.
   kurlanassociates.com/understanding-the-sales-force/2018/new-data-shows-how-
   relationships-and-the-need-to-be-liked-impact-sales-performance/.

5. *Seinfeld*, season 4, episode 23, "The Pilot," *Seinfeld*, directed by Tom Cherones, written
   by Larry David, Jerry Seinfeld, and Peter Mehlman, aired May 20, 1993, https://www
   .imdb.com/title/tt0697754/quotes/?ref_=tt_trv_qu.

CHAPTER 8: TRUST THE PROCESS (WHAT WOULD BOB ROSS DO?)

1. Michael J. Mooney, "Why Is Bob Ross Still So Popular?," *The Atlantic*, July 28, 2020,
   https://www.theatlantic.com/culture/archive/2020/07/why-bob-ross-still-so-popular
   /614431/.

2. "If You Build It, He Will Come," *Field of Dreams*, directed by Phil Alden Robinson
   (1989; Gordon Company), https://www.youtube.com/watch?v=5Ay5GqJwHF8.

CHAPTER 9: SALES TRAINING IN TODAY'S MARKETPLACE

1. "82% of B2B Decision-Makers Think Sales Reps Are Unprepared," SalesLion, accessed March 14, 2024, https://saleslion.io/sales-statistics/82-of-b2b-decision-makers-think-sales-reps-are-unprepared/#:~:text=However%2C%20according%20to%20a%20survey,damage%20to%20a%20company's%20reputation.

2. "149 Eye-Opening Sales Statistics to Consider in 2024 (by Category)," SPOTIO, January 9, 2024, https://spotio.com/blog/sales-statistics/.

3. Marcus Sheridan, "The Sales Problem Everyone Ignores: An Untrained Sales Force," iMPACT, January 22, 2024, https://www.impactplus.com/blog/lack-of-sales-training#:~:text=The%20entire%20sales%20industry%20is,self%2Dtaught%20social%20sellers.%E2%80%9D.

4. Vala Afshar, "How High Performing Sales Teams Use Technology to Win in Today's Economy," *ZDNET*, December 12, 2022, https://www.zdnet.com/article/how-high-performing-sales-teams-use-technology-to-win-in-todays-economy/.

5. N. Mrázová, "You Are Coaching Your Reps Wrong. These Unconventional Strategies Will Return $29 Per Each $1 Invested," CloudTalk, December 1, 2023, https://www.cloudtalk.io/blog/you-are-coaching-your-reps-wrong-these-unconventional-strategies-will-return-29-per-each-1-invested/.

CHAPTER 10: SALES LEADERSHIP VS. SALES MANAGEMENT

1. Orianna Rosa Royle, "Nearly All Bosses Are 'Accidental' with No Formal Training—and Research Shows It's Leading 1 in 3 Workers to Quit," *Fortune*, October 16, 2023, https://fortune.com/europe/2023/10/16/bosses-accidental-formal-training-workers-quit-cmi/.

2. "Taking Responsibility—Why UK PLC Needs Better Managers," Chartered Management Institute, October 2023, pp. 9, 13, https://www.managers.org.uk/wp-content/uploads/2023/10/CMI_BMB_GoodManagment_Report.pdf.

3. Cheryl Powers, "How Your Sales Managers Are Keeping You From Having the Business You Deserve—Part 1," LinkedIn article, December 9, 2015, https://www.linkedin.com/pulse/how-your-sales-managers-keeping-you-from-having-business-powers/.

4. "Men don't follow titles, they follow courage," *Braveheart*, directed by Mel Gibson (1995; Icon Productions and The Ladd Company), https://www.youtube.com/watch?v=5kjQxpoSlzc.

INDEX

transparent leadership, 62–63
trial closes, 52
turnover rate (churn), 68–69

U

unrealistic expectations, 35–36
upfront contract technique, 6–7, 50

V

validating assessments, 124
value, providing, 90–91

W

Wallace, William, 175
weather-forecast analogy, 16–17

Weiss, David, 58
"why change" message, 58
Will to Sell metric, The Sales DNA
    Test, 125–128
  commitment, 126
  desire, 125–126
  motivation, 127
  outlook, 126–127
  responsibility, 127–128
Williams, Serena, 179
win stage, sales process, 142–143
Winnett, Mike, 49
Wolf of Wall Street, The (movie), 4–5
Woodworth's Personal Data Sheet, 111

ABOUT THE AUTHOR

AT A YOUNG AGE, STEVE HEROUX had debilitating anxiety at the mere thought of standing in front of the class and giving a book report. But thanks to the accidental discovery of his first sales job selling Cutco knives at eighteen years old, he later became the #1 Cutco rep in the United States in his senior year of college. After seven years of performing at a high level in both sales and sales leadership roles with Cutco, he decided he wanted a new challenge and entered the insurance field. He went on to have an extensively successful career at Aflac, as a sales leader and salesperson, where he became the #1 agent in a field of more than 60,000 agents.

The more he immersed himself in this world, the more he realized something was fundamentally wrong. The techniques being taught were relics of a bygone era, designed for a world that no longer existed. They were focused on manipulation rather than collaboration, on coercion rather than inspiration. He saw talented individuals struggle under the weight of these antiquated methods. He saw teams falter, not because of a lack of effort or skill, but because they were being led astray by principles that had outlived their usefulness. And he knew something had to change. He realized that there were countless people whose lives and businesses could be positively impacted if they simply had the chance to thrive in the right environments. For this reason, among many others, he started The Sales Collective to help both salespeople and leaders develop the qualities and mindset to drive transformational change.

Made in United States
Cleveland, OH
16 February 2025

14419820R00121